Teaching Physical Edu
Children with Special
Needs and Disabilities

CH00420491

Teaching Physical Education to Children with Special Educational Needs and Disabilities provides a thorough overview of the challenges and opportunities for inclusion in PE lessons. Combining a theoretical framework with practical strategies for teachers, the title covers a diverse range of issues which teachers need to address to provide high quality learning experiences for children with SEND.

This second edition is grounded in up-to-date research on inclusion and has been fully updated in line with the SEND Code of Practice and Ofsted Inspection Framework. It seeks to demystify the statutory responsibilities placed upon teachers and schools to include children with SEND and offers practical examples of how PE teachers can make use of different strategies to differentiate through their planning and assessment. A new chapter explores the importance of consulting with and empowering children with SEND, and additional focus is given to how teachers can work together with SENCOs and LSAs to develop an inclusive culture in PE lessons.

Written in an accessible style with reflective tasks in each chapter, this unique text clearly outlines relevant practice-based evidence to fully include children with SEND in PE lessons. This will be essential reading for teachers and school leaders and will enable PE teachers to plan and deliver inclusive lessons for all children.

Philip Vickerman is Pro Vice Chancellor for Strategic Initiatives and Professor of Inclusive Education at Liverpool John Moores University, UK.

Anthony Maher is a Senior Lecturer in Physical Education and Youth Sport at Edge Hill University, UK.

Teaching Physical Education to Children with Special Educational Needs and Disabilities

Second Edition

Philip Vickerman and
Anthony Maher

Routledge
Taylor & Francis Group

LONDON AND NEW YORK

Second edition published 2019
by Routledge
2 Park Square, Milton Park, Abingdon, Oxon OX14 4RN

and by Routledge
711 Third Avenue, New York, NY 10017

Routledge is an imprint of the Taylor & Francis Group, an informa business

© 2019 Philip Vickerman and Anthony Maher

First edition published 2007 by Routledge

British Library Cataloguing in Publication Data
A catalogue record for this book is available from the British Library

Library of Congress Cataloging in Publication Data
Names: Vickerman, Philip, 1968- author. | Maher, A., author.
Title: Teaching physical education to children with special educational
    needs and disabilities / Philip Vickerman and Anthony Maher.
Description: Second edition. | New York : Routledge, 2019. | "First
    edition published 2007 by Routledge"—T.p. verso.
Identifiers: LCCN 2018013411 (print) | LCCN 2018015457
    (ebook) | ISBN 9781351206150 (ebook) | ISBN 9780815383345
    (Hardback) | ISBN 9780815383352 (Paperback) | ISBN
    9781351206150 (Ebook)
Subjects: LCSH: Physical education for children with disabilities—
    Great Britain.
Classification: LCC GV245 (ebook) | LCC GV245 .V53 2019 (print)
    | DDC 371.9/04486—dc23
LC record available at https://lccn.loc.gov/2018013411

ISBN: 978-0-8153-8334-5 (hbk)
ISBN: 978-0-8153-8335-2 (pbk)
ISBN: 978-1-351-20615-0 (ebk)

Typeset in Garamond
by Swales & Willis Ltd, Exeter, Devon, UK

MIX
Paper from
responsible sources
FSC
www.fsc.org   FSC® C013056

Printed and bound in Great Britain by
TJ International Ltd, Padstow, Cornwall

Phil: This book is dedicated to my wife Heather, and children, Liam and Hannah.

Anthony: For Katherine, Caleb, and Isla.

Contents

Tasks

Preface

One in five children in England and Wales is now identified as having a SEND, and consequently teachers of PE are facing daily challenges to facilitate pupils' accessibility and entitlement to inclusion within mainstream school contexts. Offering a combination of theoretical and practical strategies to include children with SEND within lessons, this unique title:

- directly applies current research to the practice of including children with SEND in PE;
- offers an outline of the statutory responsibilities placed upon teachers and schools to include children with SEND in PE;
- covers a diverse range of issues, which teachers need to address in order to provide high quality learning experiences for children with SEND;
- includes a series of reflective tasks, extended reading and further contacts within each chapter to assist with the development of knowledge and understanding of SEND and PE.

This authoritative book offers an opportunity to explore in depth the complexities of including children with SEND in PE. This is an extensive resource that requires no prior knowledge of the topic and is essential reading for practitioners who want to involve *all* children in physical activities and education.

Is a second edition really needed?

Over a decade has passed since *Teaching Physical Education to Children with Special Educational Needs* was accepted for publication. During this time, there have been a number of significant changes and developments, both nationally and internationally, in policies and practices relating to teacher education, pedagogy, and supporting children with SEND. Two of the most significant examples in Britain include the introduction of a new National Curriculum and a new SEND Code of Practice, both of which have influenced the way local authorities and schools develop and implement provision aimed at facilitating the inclusion of children with SEND. These developments, together with significant structural changes to teacher training in Britain, have impacted on the ways in which teachers are prepared for a career that involves including children with SEND.

The contribution of academics to the wider debate about issues associated with teaching physical education to children with SEND has also increased since the publication of the first edition of this book. Indeed, there is now an ever growing body of literature focusing on inclusion and special educational needs from the perspective of teachers, teacher educators, special educational needs coordinators, learning supports assistants, parents, and children. While the new edition will continue to provide a valuable resource for serving and in-service teachers, it will also speak to university students, researchers, and academics interested in special needs education and inclusive physical education.

What's new in this book?

No core content has been removed from the first edition. However, all redundant policies and guidance has either been removed or updated depending on its relevance to teaching and schooling. Moreover, out-of-date literature and research has been replaced by more contemporary sources to ensure that the academic underpinning has currency. In addition, reflective tasks, further readings and practice-based evidence now reflect changes to teacher education, and is aligned with the Teachers' Standards to ensure relevance and applicability. A notable addition to this book is a chapter (Chapter 9) relating to seeking and valuing the voices of children with SEND. Furthermore, Chapter 7, which focuses on 'Multidisciplinary approaches and working in partnership', has undergone significant revision and now includes lengthy sections relating to working in partnership with special educational needs coordinators and learning support assistants, given the importance of both for developing an inclusive culture in PE.

Abbreviations

ADHD	Attention deficit hyperactivity disorder
AfPE	Association for Physical Education
BAALPE	British Association of Advisers and Lecturers in Physical Education
CPD	Continuing professional development
DCD	Development Co-ordination Disorder
DCMS	Department for Culture, Media and Sport
DES	Department of Education and Science
DfE	Department for Education
DfEE	Department for Education and Employment
DfES	Department for Education and Skills
DoE	Department of Education
DoH	Department of Health
EAL	English as an additional language
EFDS	English Federation for Disability Sport
IEP	Individual education plan
ITT	Initial teacher training
LEA	Local education authority
LSA	Learning support assistants
NC	National Curriculum
NDSO	National disability sport organisation
NQT	Newly qualified teacher
OFSTED	Office for Standards in Education
PCE	Postgraduate Certificate in Education
PE	Physical education
PEA (UK)	Physical Education Association (United Kingdom)
PESSCL	PE, School Sport and Club Links
QCA	Qualification Curriculum Authority
QTS	Qualified teacher status
SENCO	Special educational needs co-ordinator
SEND	Special educational needs and disabilities
SLT	Senior leadership team

TDA	Teacher Development Agency
TTA	Teacher Training Agency
UCET	Universities Council for the Education of Teachers
UNESCO	United Nations Educational, Cultural and Scientific Organization
YST	Youth Sport Trust

Chapter 1

The context for inclusion

Introduction and purpose of the book

Teaching is often referred to as both an art and a science and consequently requires a combination of creativity and innovation, matched by theoretical reflection and refinement. This book aims to address this eclectic approach to teaching children with special educational needs and disabilities (SEND) in the physical education (PE) curriculum. The book will discuss and debate what can be considered as the essential theoretical elements of teaching children with SEND in PE, whilst offering opportunities for reflection on how these can be delivered in practice. In addition, the book encourages you to 'think out of the box', be open to change, have open minds, and have high expectations of children with SEND and what they can achieve in PE, school sport and lifelong learning and participation in physical activity.

Whilst there is no one correct way of teaching, or set of skills, techniques or protocols to follow, the book does set out to establish what can be considered as core principles of good practice. In order for you to ensure children with SEND have positive, meaningful, and successful learning experiences in PE, you as an individual teacher need to combine these core principles with your own individual uniqueness and experiences to produce the right mix for successful learning.

It is our intention that this book will act as a stimulus for thought and reflection, whatever stage of personal and professional development you are at (i.e. whether you are a trainee teacher, recently qualified, experienced practitioner, or working in an advisory or leadership capacity). Furthermore, the book will be of relevance to academics and those with a general interest in the area of disability sport, and can be used as an opportunity to reflect on and review your current knowledge, understanding and delivery practices.

The book is structured around themed chapters that combine academic theory, research, practical application, reflective tasks and further reading. It is envisaged that this diverse approach will meet the individual needs of readers, whatever their stage of development. As a result, the book sets out to:

- draw upon current research evidence and apply this to the practice of including children with SEND in PE;
- examine the statutory responsibilities that are placed upon teachers in relation to including children with SEND;
- combine academic theory with opportunities for critical reflection;
- provide a comprehensive range of tasks, issues and points for further debate;
- equip you with the knowledge, skills and understanding to ensure that children with SEND in PE learn and develop effectively.

The rise of the political and statutory inclusion agenda

In October 1997 the new Labour Government launched their Green Paper on special needs education, which stated:

> We want to see more pupils with special educational needs (SEN) included within mainstream primary and secondary schools. We support the United Nations Educational, Scientific and Cultural Organization (UNESCO) Salamanca World Statement on Special Needs Education 1994. This calls on governments to adopt the principle of inclusive education, enrolling all children in regular schools, unless there are compelling reasons for doing otherwise. This implies a progressive extension of the capacity of mainstream schools to provide for children with a wide range of needs.
>
> (DfEE 1997a: 44)

The return of the Labour Government to power in 1997, saw inclusion rise up the political and statutory agenda in the United Kingdom (UK) to such an extent that there was widespread evidence of policies embedded across diverse sectors of society. In education, for example, there was an increased emphasis on the inclusion of children with SEND through legislation such as the National Curriculum (NC) (2000) Inclusion Statement (QCA 1999c), SEN and Disability Rights Act (DfES 2001c) and the revised *Code of Practice* (DfES 2001b). In addition, the introduction of the Human Rights Act (Her Majesty's Stationery Office, 1998) and the Government's *Every Child Matters* (DfES 2004a) agenda focused attention even more on the rights and responsibilities relating to children with SEND.

The UK-based picture mirrored similar developments in the USA associated with concepts of 'zero reject' and 'entitlement for all'. For example, the 'Public Law 94—142 Education for All Handicapped Children Act (1975)' in the USA set out to ensure children were given a fundamental right to access education, and have a clear statement of their SEND, which was subject to regular review. The law also enforced a requirement for states and localities to assess and ensure the effectiveness of their efforts to educate so-called 'handicapped' children. Consequently, those responsible for the education of these children became accountable for the development and implementation of an appropriate education, within a context that was mindful of pupils' individual needs. Furthermore, many European countries established similar statutory expectations on the inclusion of children with SEND which affirms the social drive for children to gain their entitlement and accessibility to an education which meets their individual needs.

In the UK, statistical evidence from the DfES (2004b) supported the increased emphasis on inclusion, and showed year-on-year rises in the number of children with SEND (i.e. registered on the Code of Practice) being included within mainstream education (2004 – 76 per cent, 2001 – 61 per cent, 1997 – 57 per cent, 1993 – 48 per cent). Due to changes to SEND legislation and policy generally, and SEND classifications, assessments and support in particular, it is not possible to provide a direct comparison between current statistics and those cited from 2004. Nonetheless, the following is offered to give a flavour of the current landscape: the percentage of pupils with SEND attending state-funded primary schools has increased between 2010 and 2017, from 77.2 per cent to 82.8 per cent. However, the percentage of pupils eligible for SEN Support but without Statements or Education, Health and Care (EHC) plans attending state-funded secondary schools has declined over the same period, from 72.4 per cent in 2010 to 56.6 per cent in 2017 (DfE 2017a). Importantly, these numbers do not include children who attend independent schools. Nonetheless, there remains pressure on teacher educators, schools and teachers to reflect upon these issues because, as the NC (2014) states, teachers must (1) promote the spiritual, moral, cultural, mental and physical development of *all pupils*; and (2) prepare *all pupils* for the opportunities, responsibilities and experiences of later life (DfE 2014a).

According to Avramadis and Norwich (2002), teachers are recognised as the main agents of the implementation of inclusive policy and, as such, 'without a coherent plan for teacher training in the educational needs of children with SEN, attempts to include these children in the mainstream would be difficult' (Avramadis and Norwich 2002: 139). Indeed, much of the available research relating to PE teacher training emphasises a perceived failure – expressed mainly by the teachers themselves – of the British Government and teacher educators to providing training that enables them to teach pupils with SEND in PE (Vickerman 2007; Vickerman and Coates 2009).

Therefore, there is an obvious need for agencies such as initial teacher training (ITT) providers, schools and teachers to review existing practices and procedures in order to provide a systematic approach to this area of their work. In this respect, it is important to note that special educational needs coordinators (SENCOs) and learning support assistants (LSAs) have highlighted the challenges associated with inclusion in PE in particular, citing the training of teachers and their own opportunities for professional development as being limiting factors (Maher 2016). This is significant given that SENCOs and LSAs are supposed to be key facilitators of inclusion.

In order for change to have impact, Depauw and Doll-Tepper (2000) argued for the need to recognise inclusion as a process model in which associated issues are infused throughout all of the teaching, learning, policy and practice aspects of your work. In other words, a holistic and possibly quite radical approach is required. Therefore, in order to produce positive PE experiences for children with SEND it is vital not merely to address issues at a superficial level, but more essentially to make a difference through inclusive delivery in practice. This book will help you to meet these expectations through a combination of theory, reflection and practical examples of including children with SEND in PE.

Setting high expectations

In order to reflect a commitment to inclusion at government level, the latest NC (DfE 2014a) and the Teachers' Standards (DfE 2013a), which set the minimum requirements for teachers' conduct and practice, emphasise the important of setting high expectations which inspire, motivate and challenge all pupils, including those with SEND. This view is rooted in the 1994 Salamanca Statement (UNESCO 1994), which identified a set of beliefs and proclamations relating to the notion that every child has a fundamental right to education. It identified core principles of providing children with the opportunity to learn, an education system designed to take account of diversity, access to regular child-centred education and the acceptance of inclusive orientation as a means of combating discrimination and building an inclusive society.

Task 1.1   The Salamanca Statement

Reflect on the 1994 Salamanca Statement (UNESCO 1994), which establishes a set of beliefs and proclamations related to the notion that every child has a fundamental right to education. The statement identifies what are considered to be core principles of providing children with the **opportunity to learn, establishment of high standards, an education system designed to take account of diversity, access to regular child-centred education, and acceptance of inclusive orientation as a means of combating discrimination to build an inclusive society.** Using the table below, analyse what you understand by these terms, and how you can ensure they are delivered as part of your daily teaching and learning practice.

Key aspects of the Salamanca Statement (1994)	What do you understand the key aspect to be referring to, and how can you ensure this is delivered as part of your daily practice?
Providing children with an opportunity to learn	• understanding the individual needs of children; • matching my teaching to the needs of children; • being prepared to adapt and modify my teaching; • listening to the views of colleagues and working in partnership; • baseline assessments and ongoing review and evaluation of my teaching.
Establishing high standards and expectations of children with SEND Creating an education system designed to take account of diversity Access to regular child-centred education Acceptance of inclusion as a means of combating discrimination	

Through the introduction of recent inclusive legislation within the UK the notion of education for all, and entitlement, are viewed as central to the Government's drive to create a socially inclusive society in which all children are able to participate, learn and reach their full potential.

NC Inclusion Statement

The NC 2014 states that every state-funded school must offer a curriculum that is broad, balanced and which:

• promotes the spiritual, moral, cultural, mental and physical development of pupils at the school and of society, and
• prepares pupils at the school for the opportunities, responsibilities and experiences of later life.

(DfE 2014a: 4)

Significantly, like its predecessors, the statutory curriculum includes an inclusion statement. Here, the onus is placed on teachers to plan and deliver lessons in ways that ensure that there are no barriers to pupil achievement. According to this document, teachers should recognise the individual learning needs of each pupil, ensuring that potential areas of difficulty are highlighted and supported, so that pupils with SEND can study every national curriculum subject (DfE 2014a). In this respect, the *Code of Practice* (DfE/DoH 2015) provides statutory guidance to schools and teachers on duties, policies and procedures relating to Part 3 of the Children and Families Act 2014 and associated regulations. Thus, it is important that you refer to the Code in order to understand your legal duties to children with SEND. As the DfE/DoH (2015: 12) state:

> whenever they [schools and teachers] are taking decisions they must give consideration to what the Code says. They cannot ignore it. They must fulfil their statutory duties towards children and young people with SEN or disabilities in the light of the guidance set out in it. They must be able to demonstrate in their arrangements for children and young people with SEN or disabilities that they are fulfilling their statutory duty to have regard to the Code.

The new Code was released in an attempt to make the SEND system more efficient and effective for parents and children. A pledge was included to identify SEND at the earlier possible opportunity so that learning needs could be supported, together with a commitment to involve parents in key decisions relating to the supported offered to their child (DfE/DoH 2015). This is important given the link between early identification of learning needs such as dyslexia (e.g. Snowling 2012) and autism spectrum conditions (ASC) (Boyd et al. 2010), and the appropriateness of learning support and educational outcomes. An increase in responsibilities for teachers and other support staff such as LSAs and SENCOs means that changes from the 2001 Code should be acknowledged and understood. Below is a list of some of the key changes evident in the new Code, which reflect the Children and Families Act 2014:

The *Code of Practice* (2015) covers the 0–25 age range and includes guidance relating to disabled children and young people as well as those with SEND

- more emphasis on the involvement of children and parents in decision-making at individual and strategic levels;
- a stronger focus on high aspirations and on improving outcomes for children;
- includes guidance on the joint planning and commissioning of services to ensure close co-operation between education, health and social care;
- includes guidance on publishing a Local Offer of support for children with SEND;
- new guidance for education and training settings on taking a graduated approach to identifying and supporting pupils and students with SEND (replaces School Action and School Action Plus);
- for children with more complex needs, a coordinated assessment process and the new 0–25 Education, Health and Care plan (EHC plan) replace Statements and Learning Difficulty Assessments (LDAs);

- greater focus on support that enables those with SEN to succeed in their education and make a successful transition to adulthood;
- information is provided on relevant duties under the Equality Act 2010;
- information is provided on relevant provisions of the Mental Capacity Act 2005;
- new guidance on supporting children with SEND who are in youth custody.

(DfE/DoH 2015: 14)

For a detailed explanation of these changes, and what they mean for children, parents and schools, please read *Everybody Included: The SEND Code of Practice Explained* (Nasen 2014). In addition, Massey's (2016) *Provision Mapping and the SEND Code of Practice* offers a useful resource to assist teachers to evidence the support they have provided pupils with SEND and the impact that support has had on learning and educational outcomes.

Task 1.2   The Teachers' Standards

Look at five of the Teachers' Standards (DfE 2013a) identified below and reflect upon how you can meet these when including children with SEND in PE. Also take time to consider how you could evidence that these Standards had been met.

In summary, it is essential teachers understand and engage with the NC inclusion statement, SEN *Code of Practice* and Teachers' Standards to ensure that they fulfil their legal responsibility of creating inclusive lessons that meet the needs and capitalise on the capabilities of all pupils, especially those with SEND.

Standard	Mechanisms to ensure it is met in practice
Set high expectations, which inspire, motivate and challenge pupils (with SEND)	
Promote good progress and outcomes by pupils (with SEND)	
Plan and teach well-structured lessons (to pupils with SEND)	
Adapt teaching to respond to the strengths and needs (of pupils with SEND)	
Make accurate and productive use of assessment (for pupils with SEND)	

The role of statutory and non-statutory agencies in supporting the inclusion agenda

The DfE is a government department responsible for education and children's services in England. It is also home to the Government Equalities Office, which is responsible for equality strategy and legislation across government. According to the DfE (2017b), 'we work to provide children's services and education that ensure opportunity is equal for all, no matter what their background or family circumstances'. Thus, through a range of legislative and policy-making strategies, they play a central role in setting the agenda for others in the delivery of education, PE and SEND.

In relation to teacher education and the inspection of standards, the National College for Teaching and Leadership (NCTL) and Office for Standards in Education (OFSTED) play central roles in ensuring teachers are adequately prepared to include children with SEND. The NCTL (2017) aims to improve academic standards by recruiting and developing teachers to meet the demands of their multifarious roles and responsibilities.

In conjunction with this remit, the NCTL are responsible for recognising teachers' professional competencies for the award of qualified teacher status (QTS). The aim is to ensure that teachers are competently prepared through their ITT and future professional development training to maximise the learning and development that takes place with children, including those with SEND, in schools. In addition, through setting benchmark standards, they seek to ensure that teachers of the future have sufficient training and development opportunities to support children with SEND effectively once they are working in schools (NCTL 2017).

In contrast, the role of OFSTED is to: 'raise standards and improve lives' through inspecting and regulating services that provide education and skills to learners' (OFSTED 2017). Therefore, in the context of the training that takes place in ITT institutions, they are responsible for inspecting and reporting upon the quality and standards of delivery by these providers. When it comes to what OFSTED should do during a school visit, the *School Inspection Handbook* states that 'Inspectors will evaluate evidence relating to the achievement of specific groups of pupils and individuals, including . . . pupils who have special educational needs and/or disabilities' (OFSTED 2016: 24). It is worth noting that pupils with SEND feature prominently in the grade descriptors used by OFSTED to rate schools.

The professional PE associations and disability sport organisations

The professional PE associations and disability sport organisations are central to the successful implementation of the inclusion of children with SEND, from policy through to practice levels. Although the Association for Physical

Education (AfPE) does not have any statutory powers and responsibilities, its members play a vital role in ensuring that teachers are adequately prepared and supported to deliver the inclusive agenda within PE and school sport. They also play a key role in lobbying government and statutory agencies for effective change or guidance in order to ensure that current educational agendas are sufficiently met. In addition, they seek to produce resources and documentation that will assist their members to support children with SEND.

In contrast, the English Federation for Disability Sport (EFDS) aims to serve as the main supporting and coordinating body for the development of sport for people with disabilities through working with Sport England, the National Disability Sport Organisations (NDSOs) for specific impairment groups, National Governing Bodies (NGBs) of sport, regional coaching and education networks, including the County Sports Partnerships, clubs and schools (EFDS 2017). Thus, EFDS has a central role to play in both lobbying and supporting PE and school sports agencies to deliver the Government's inclusion agenda and offer specialist advice, support and guidance to agencies and individuals.

Over time, the Youth Sport Trust (YST) has come to play and important role in PE generally, and attempts to create a more inclusive culture in the subject in particular. For example, the YST worked in partnership with the EFDS and Sainsbury's to develop the Active Kids for All Inclusive PE training to ensure that trainee and in-service teachers have the knowledge and practical skills to include all pupils in curriculum PE (YST 2017a). YST also offer free online resources to schools and teachers to support their attempts to plan and deliver lessons that meet the needs and optimise the capabilities of pupils with SEND. TOP Sportsability is one such programme providing free resources to teachers, LSAs and other sports practitioners. This aims to:

- provide physical activity and sport options for young people with high support needs;
- create a vehicle for the inclusion of disabled and non-disabled young people together;
- provide a basic introduction to a wide range of sports and activities in support of the School Games programme.

(YST 2017b)

Government legislation and regulation linked to SEND and teachers

Historically, the UK Government has supported and maintained through legislation and policies a significant infrastructure of segregated schools. However, there is a long-established tradition of encouraging mainstream schools to make some form of provision that was recognisably 'special', and guidance has been offered as to what this provision should consist of. It is not only in ITT that the government has set out policies, but over many years conventional expectations for the provision of schooling for children with SEND have been apparent.

Since the emergence of the first significant (in terms of SEND) piece of educational legislation with the 1944 Education Act (DoE 1944), it is only in more recent times through introduction of the NC (QCA 1999a) and the 02/02 (TTA 2002) standards for the award of QTS that some synergy of policy in education in schools, and education in ITT related to inclusion has begun to emerge. Thus, in order for the Government's inclusion agenda to become a reality in schools, there is a need to ensure that the policies and agendas of respective agencies work in tandem, to complement, rather than work against, each other. For example, as the NC (2014) continued to empha-sise SEND and inclusion, this should also be reflected in an increased emphasis within the Teachers' Standards.

The 1944 Education Act (DoE 1944) was the first piece of legislation that established separate schooling for pupils of different aptitudes and abilities. These were established through separate forms of special education with dif-ferent types of schools for different forms of disability related to a total of 11 medically defined categories of handicap (Fredrickson and Cline 2002). However, the Act placed a duty on local education authorities (LEAs) of the time to ascertain the needs of children with SEND, and anticipated that treat-ment in many cases may be best served in mainstream education.

The reality for many teachers training to work in mainstream schools, how-ever, was that the issue of disability, and the education of such children, were rarely addressed. At the time, this was seen as the role of special school teachers, who had the knowledge to work with such pupils, rather than educating them alongside their non-disabled peers, where mainstream teachers were ill equipped to support them. This situation remained largely unchanged until the publica-tion of the Warnock Report in 1978 (DES 1978), which acknowledged that around 18 per cent of school pupils could be expected to have special needs, and reinforced that the majority of these needs should be met in the mainstream.

This change in policy, culminating in the 1981 Education Act (DES 1981), in which 'statementing' (a formal process of identifying, assessing and supporting a child with SEND) was introduced, brought more mainstream teachers into contact with children with SEND. In conjunction with this requirement, there was no formal ITT stipulation for teachers to be trained to support this goal. Consequently, as more children with SEND were inte-grated into mainstream schools, few if any teachers or training providers had spent time adequately considering the needs of these children. As a result, the changing policy directives reflected in schools were not being developed alongside changes in ITT provision, thus demonstrating a distinct lack of co-ordination and multi-agency working.

In 1994, the *Code of Practice on the Identification and Assessment of Special Educational Needs* (DoE 1994) was introduced, which brought with it a designation of clear roles and responsibilities that schools must adopt in order to support children with SEND. This was replaced by the 2001 *Code of Practice* and, more recently, a 2015 version. The 2015 *Code of Practice* takes account of the 2001 SEN and Disability Act, the 2010 Equality Act, and the 2014 Children and Families Act, and puts a stronger emphasis on children with SEND being educated in the mainstream. In addition, rights of statutory assessment and duties of local education authorities to arrange services to support parents and help resolve any matters of conflict have been further emphasised. Thus, with the increasing emphasis of inclusion being placed upon schools, the need to ensure teachers are given the appropriate training in ITT is self-evident, and is reflected (although only minimally) in the Teachers' Standards that are used for the award of QTS.

Task 1.3   Developing a cohesive framework for inclusive PE

Reflect upon what you would see as the positive features of establishing a cohesive framework to support PE teachers to deliver inclusion for children with SEND. As part of your analysis you should look at what you understand by the different roles each agency (i.e. DfE, OFSTED, NCTL, ITT providers, and professional PE and disability associations) play in ensuring pupils with SEND receive positive experiences in PE.

Thus, the need for government educational policy within schools to match the ITT policy can be seen as a critical success factor in ensuring that the needs of children with SEND in mainstream schools are adequately met. This further strengthened the need for agencies such as DfE, OFSTED, NCTL, and ITT providers to work together within a cohesive framework to support PE teachers to deliver inclusion for children with SEND.

Agency	What role do you see the agencies playing in order to provide a cohesive framework for inclusive PE?
Department for Education (DfE)	
Office for Standards in Education (OFSTED)	
National College for Teaching and Leadership (NCTL)	
ITT providers	
Professional PE Associations (Association for PE)	
English Federation for Disability Sport (EFDS)	

Implementing teacher training and SEND policy in practice: multi-agency approach to a multi-agency challenge for PE teachers?

In her foreword for the White Paper Educational Excellence, the Secretary of State for Education, Nicky Morgan, said 'Education has the power to transform lives and, for me, is a matter of social justice – extending opportunity to every child' (Morgan 2016: 3). The Government, DfE and agencies like the NCTL and OFSTED, play a critical role in ensuring that partnership, collaboration and joined-up thinking are fostered in order to ensure that future generations of PE teachers are equipped to deliver the Government's objective of a truly world-class education system, which includes meeting fully the needs of children with SEND.

Specifically, in relation to children with SEND in school contexts, the DfE (2016) have stated that Ofsted and the Care Quality Commission will begin to inspect local area implementation from May 2016, focusing on how well the needs of children with SEND are identified and met, and how well local agencies (including health and social care) work together to do so. Whilst this brings with it further regulation and monitoring of schools, it does give all stakeholders the opportunity to measure the extent to which progress is being made to support children with SEND.

Whilst OFSTED do not make a separate judgement on SEND provision, instead opting to consider it as part of the whole-school assessment, inspectors must evaluate 'the extent to which the education provided by the school meets the needs of the range of pupils at the school, including pupils with disabilities and pupils with SEN' (OFSTED 2016: 34–35). This is tied into OFSTED's overall judgement of the school's overall effectiveness. Therefore, in relation to school contexts, OFSTED will examine the progress of pupils with SEND by comparing them to pupils nationally with similar starting points, and examine the impact of funded support, the expectation being that 'the identification of special educational needs leads to additional or different arrangements being made and a consequent improvement in progress' (OFSTED 2016: 55).

The teacher training process from day one, through ITT, award of QTS, induction and lifelong continuing professional development

At this juncture it is important to draw attention to a significant change to the teacher training landscape, which has occurred since the publication of the first edition of this book. The UK government attempted to improve the quality of teaching and leadership in state-funded schools by devolving responsibility to schools to lead and manage teacher training (DfE 2013b). This was a significant step-change from the previous focus on university-led provision. Of the 1,224 PE teacher training places allocated for the 2015–2016 academic year in England, the majority were school (n = 720) rather than university (n = 504) led (NCTL 2016). One outcome of the changing landscape of teacher education is that the many of those who aspire to enter the PE teaching profession undergo a non-QTS undergraduate PE degree before a one-year school-centred initial teacher training (SCITT) placement at a government-approved school (DfE, 2014c). Therefore, the onus is on universities and schools to ensure that aspiring PE teachers are prepared for their role as inclusive educators. It is too early to assess the impact of this change on the extent to which PE teachers have the knowledge, skills, experience, and confidence to teach pupils with SEND. Nonetheless, there was a notable body of research suggesting that PE teachers were entering the profession under-prepared for their role as inclusive educators (see Vickerman and Coates 2009; Vickerman 2007). In this regard, Morley et al. (2017) have explored the use of online resources, Maher et al. (2017) have analysed the impact of placement in a special school, and Sparkes et al. (2017) have used simulation as a form of embodied pedagogy, all in an attempt to understand how best to prepare wannabe PE teachers, all of whom are studying non-QTS courses, to teach pupils with SEND. Indeed, it has become increasingly important for those aspiring teachers who choose a SCITT route into teaching to develop a positive attitude to inclusion, be aware of their legal obligations to pupils with SEND, and have experience planning and delivering inclusive lessons (ideally to pupils with SEND), amongst other things, because these important issues will not be sufficiently covered by schools.

This book will support teacher professional develop and growth in this respect. However, it is important to acknowledge that the teaching profession is based upon 'reflective practice', and that teachers' knowledge and understanding develop and grow over a lifetime of work with children (with SEND). As a consequence, in relation to teachers of PE, it is important to recognise that training in inclusive education for children with SEND must involve several agencies working together in partnership to ensure that learning and development processes work effectively throughout a teacher's career.

The DfE, NCTL, and OFSTED advocate that the Teachers' Standards will be the main vehicle for measuring and increasing competence within ITT. The Teachers' Standards, which have statutory force, define the minimum practice required by trainees for the award of QTS (DfE 2013a). PE ITT providers and schools must use the standards to assess when, if at all, trainee teachers should be recommended for the award of QTS. The Standards can also be used by teachers as a resource to support their own professional development, and by senior leaders in schools to improve standards by setting minimum expectations and assessing performance (DfE 2014b). There is an expectation that trainee and in-service teachers will understand the factors that restrict pupil learning, and know when and how to differentiate appropriately, using strategies that enable pupils to be taught effectively, especially those with SEND (DfE 2013a). Thus, ITT providers and trainee teachers need to ensure that they are both meeting the requirements of the standards, and in turn be able to demonstrate that they are competently prepared to support children with SEND.

Questions still remain as to the extent of student trainees' knowledge relating to SEND, and the appropriateness of the standards that have been identified as essential prerequisites prior to qualifying. Therefore, whilst standards give the general area to be developed, it is a matter of professional judgement by the ITT provider and schools as to how this is achieved, and the extent to which competence has been attained. In addition, there is much debate around the use of terms such as 'competence' and how this can be clearly demonstrated, interpreted and evidenced within ITT programmes (Maher et al. 2017).

Conclusion

The Teachers' Standards (DfE 2013a) for the award of QTS goes some way towards ensuring teachers have high expectations of all pupils including those with SEND; promote positive values; understand their responsibilities under the *Code of Practice;* differentiate teaching; and respond to a diverse range of learning needs. As noted at the start of this chapter, the inclusion of children with SEND and the development of quality learning experiences in PE has risen up both the statutory and political agenda. There is now a whole raft of policy expectations that are placed on trainee teachers, experienced practitioners and those with a vested interest in the education of children with SEND. Teaching is a profession that requires you to reflect upon your knowledge, understanding and personal commitment to maximise opportunities for children with SEND to be engaged in positive PE experiences. The following chapters will begin to address some of the key aspects of your training and continuing professional development that aim to prepare you for ensuring children with SEND have teachers with high expectations of them, whilst matching the curriculum to their specific needs. As a consequence, in addition to fulfilling the statutory expectations placed upon trainee and qualified PE teachers, a readiness to be flexible, open to change and responsive to the needs of individual pupils with SEND can be seen as central to successful learning experiences.

Chapter 2

Children with special educational needs and disabilities

Introduction

This chapter maps the history of SEND from the position of segregation and isolation, through to the emergence, development, and future directions of the inclusion movement of today. It examines how legislation and policy directions have transformed special education, and the impact upon children, teachers, and schools. The evolution of terminology and language will also be analysed, with particular reference to its principles and implementation in practice.

The chapter does not set out to provide extensive, detailed lists of what each SEND comprises and how you should support children with their specific needs. Rather, it seeks to outline general principles and strategies for identifying and supporting children with SEND within a context of consultation and empowerment. Consequently, in relation to identifying the needs of children with SEND, if it simply came down to the provision of robotic protocols of how to support people, first it would miss the complexity of human nature, and second it would not take any account of the interrelationship of individuality, personality, uniqueness of the teacher and the child, and the environment within which you are working. Thus, the chapter seeks to identify some fundamental principles that will help you support children's learning and development in PE, whilst gaining an insight into the specific needs and support they may require.

The development of special needs education has over time produced a complex picture within which several competing theories have contributed to the modern day 'inclusive' stance. Norwich, for example, argues that 'There is no logical purity in education' (Norwich 2002: 483), rather there is 'ideological impurity', in which no single value or principle encompasses all of what is considered worthwhile. As a result, there needs to be recognition of a range of 'multiple values' (Norwich 2002: 483) through which a series of interrelated concepts and ideologies are acknowledged as contributing to contemporary views on inclusion for children with SEND.

This rather convoluted analysis of developments, definitions and interpretations of inclusion is further acknowledged by authors in works such as Armstrong et al. (2016), Barton (1997), Croll and Moses (2000), Dyson and Millward (2000), Fredrickson and Cline (2002), and Hodkinson (2005). Therefore, in the context of Norwich's view of logical impurity this reaffirms the intention of this chapter to identify general principles and strategies to support children with SEND rather than seek to produce detailed protocols of specific needs, which oversimplifies the complexity of your teaching and learning strategies and the individuality of children.

The context and emergence of inclusion

Dyson and Millward (2000) suggest the Government Green Paper on SEND (DfEE 1997a) was the first time that the UK Government had avowedly committed itself to creating an inclusive education system. This was significant in that it indicated a commitment by the Government to two central themes.

First, it 'signalled an intention to shake special needs provision out of the somewhat complacent state in which, it is arguable, it had rested for the past two decades' (Dyson and Millward 2000: 1). For example, since the introduction of the Warnock Report in 1978 (DES 1978), culminating in the 1981 Education Act (DES 1981), the notion of children with SEND moving from special into mainstream schools was largely taken for granted. Progress during the period from 1978 to 1997 was, in Dyson and Millward's (2000) view, *ad hoc* in that it supported integration but gave no firm steer to how LEAs should implement this. This is broadly in line with policy developments in ITT in which, prior to the 4/98 (DfES 1998a) and 02/02 Professional Standards Framework (TTA 2002), guidance was given through a series of Government circulars (i.e. 3/84, 24/89, 9/92, 10/97), but with no firm instructions in relation to SEND. Consequently, some local education authorities moved further than others and, as a result, since the introduction of the 1981 Education Act there had been little in the way of a significant shift towards a more integrated system.

Second, the 1997 Green Paper brought alignment with the Salamanca Statement (UNESCO 1994), formulated in an agreement between 94 governments, and 25 international organisations. This, according to authors in an edited collection by Kiuppis and Hausstaetter (2015), recognised the extent to which inclusion had now become a 'global agenda', as well as advocating genuine recognition and commitment to 'inclusion' through cultural change. The Salamanca Statement argued:

> The challenge confronting the inclusive school is that of developing a child-centred pedagogy capable of successfully educating all children, including those who have serious disadvantages and disabilities. The merit of such schools is not only that they are capable of providing quality education for all children; their establishment is a crucial step in helping to change discriminatory attitudes, in creating welcoming communities and in developing an inclusive society.
>
> (UNESCO 1994: 6–7)

The emergence of this position is a far cry from the mid-1800s, when the first special schools were established (Fredrickson and Cline 2002). These were intended to provide for children with severe hearing or visual difficulty who could not learn in 'ordinary' schools alongside existing school provision, and places were offered only to upper and middle class pupils. In the late nineteenth century, as more children were educated from diverse backgrounds, schools were not accustomed to such diversity of learning needs. Increasing numbers of children were therefore excluded, as payment to schools at the time was 'by results'.

This rejection of children who were entitled to an education under the 1870 Education Act (DoE 1870) led to an expansion in special school provision (Fredrickson and Cline 2002). Thus, children who were perceived as 'handicapped' were seen as different from other children, and educated in separate schools. This separate provision remained largely static up until the mid-1960s when authors such as Dunn (1968) acknowledged there was a lack of evidence that children with disabilities educated in special schools did any better than those who were being educated in mainstream schools. Consequently, arguments for 'reverse separation' (Fedrickson and Cline 2002) began to emerge, prompting a move towards more 'integrated' school structures within the UK.

Task 2.1   Advantages and disadvantages of inclusive PE

Using the table below, identify what you see as the advantages and potential disadvantages of including children with SEND in mainstream PE lessons. You should consider this from three perspectives: you as the teacher, the child with SEND, and pupils without SEND.

Development of a continuum of needs

In 1970 the Education (Handicapped Children) Act (DoE 1970) removed the legal distinction between those who were, and were not educable within schools. According to Mittler (1985), this rapidly transformed the educational experience of children with SEND, including those with severe learning difficulties,

	Advantages	Potential disadvantages
Inclusive PE (pupils with and without disabilities educated alongside each other)		
Segregated PE (pupils with and without disabilities taught in separate lessons)		

and saw a growth in the skills of teachers and a development of the curriculum, in what Coupe (1986) described as the 'new special schools'. A key feature of this shift in provision was that the education of children with disabilities moved from the responsibility of government departments of health to that of education. This follows similar developments in the USA associated with concepts of 'zero reject' and 'entitlement for all'.

The principle of 'normalisation', focusing on commonalities between children rather than differences, also began to emerge with ideas that:

> the aims of education for children and young people with disabilities and other children are the same as those for all children and young people . . . Disabilities and significant difficulties do not diminish the right to and equal access to participation in society.
>
> (Inner London Education Authority 1985)

In the UK, similar developments in the Education Act 1981 (DES 1981) introduced the legally defined term SEN, following advice from the 1978 Warnock Report (DES 1978). Prior to this time, provision focused upon identifying schooling for the 'handicapped'. The Warnock Report recommended statutory categories of handicap (other than maladjustment) be abolished, and children with SEN to be identified by individual and detailed profiles of their needs following assessment. Warnock indicated that it was not appropriate to focus attention merely on a small proportion of children with severe difficulties, which gave a sharp distinction between those with and without disabilities. Thus, a child should not be assigned to a particular category, but rather SEN should be acknowledged on a continuum with so-called 'ordinary' needs. Consequently, the recommendation was made that school provision should not be either 'segregated' or 'mainstream', but on a dimension that took account of children's individual needs.

The Education Act 1981 (DES 1981) (introduced to implement the recommendations of the 1978 Warnock Report) brought a shift towards assessment of SEN, rather than the diagnosis of disability, which had been previously used to categorise, and isolate, children. This supported similar developments at the time associated with the development of 'medical and social models' of disability (Reiser and Mason 1990). Social models of disability acknowledge that once a child's individual learning needs are established through assessment, schools and teachers must respond accordingly and plan to meet their particular learning requirements. That is to say, they must make social arrangements to facilitate the learning and development of children with SEND. In contrast, 'medical models' of disability view the learning difficulty as located with the child and, as such, once assessed they would be placed into existing, unchanged provision, or placed in segregated school structures.

Focuses of causation

The location and cause of SEND has been subject to much debate (Fredrickson and Cline 2002; Farrell 2001; Lloyd 2000), and various approaches have been suggested that consider what or whom the disabling factor in a child's education is. In support of developments in medical and social models of disability, Fredrickson and Cline (2002) indicated that a combination of individual differences, environmental demands and interactional analyses have contributed to differing perspectives on the inclusion of children with SEND.

They propose that models of individual difference (medical models) are embodied in legislation prior to introduction of the Education Act 1981 (DES 1981), and are particularly emphasised in the Education Act 1944 (DoE 1944), which was dominated by disability of body or mind. Consequently, individual differences were considered along a range of biological, behavioural or cognitive domains, with causation located firmly with the child, and no acknowledgement of contributory factors external to the child, such as quality of teaching. This rather dated view is distinct from what was acknowledged in the *Code of Practice on the Identification and Assessment of Special Educational Needs* (DoE 1994), which advocated that 'schools should not automatically assume that children's learning difficulties always result solely or even mainly from problems within the child. The school's practices can make a difference – for good or ill' (DoE 1994: para. 2.19).

Therefore, teacher attitudes to inclusion and teaching pupils with SEND, the quality of teaching and learning delivered by the teacher, the ability to be equipped with the necessary knowledge and skills to support children with SEND, and school cultures are significant factors in making inclusion a success or failure (Haegele et al. 2016; Sharma and Sokal 2015; Vickerman and Coates 2009).

In contrast to medical and individual models of disability, environmental models emerged that adopted a situation-focused, rather than a person-centred focus, to inclusive provision. This suggests that SEND can only be defined in terms of relationships between what a person can do, and what a person must do to 'succeed' in any given environment. Fredrickson and Cline suggest that 'at one extreme then, the environmentally focused approach holds that there are no children with learning difficulties, only adults with teaching difficulties' (Fredrickson and Cline 2002: 40). This purview places particular importance on teachers being able to plan and deliver lessons that meet the needs and capitalise on the capabilities of pupils with SEND.

This supports the work of Seamus Hegarty who in the 1980s advocated that children should be placed on a 'continuum of provision', that should equate to discrete categories of need. As a consequence, rather than attempting to adapt the child to the environment and see the disability as located with the child (medical model), schools and teachers conversely should be looking to how they can modify their learning environments (social model) in order that it meets the individual needs of children. As a result, this necessitates schools and teachers to be prepared to think in different ways and recognise that there are many methods and strategies that can be utilised to support the inclusion of children with SEND (see Florian 2014; Mitchell 2014).

Interactional models advocate impossibility in separating the learning competencies of individual children from the environment within which they live and function. Models of disability, causation, and location are seen as a combination of complex interactions between the strengths and weaknesses of the child, levels of support available, and the appropriateness of education being provided. Thus, neither environmental nor individual approaches on their own fit the particular 'reality' of SEND in schools, and whilst the knowledge, skills and experiences of children with disabilities is embodied (Sparkes et al. 2017) – that is, in, of and through the body – learning environments and experiences are social constructs. Therefore, the extent to which pupils with SEND receive meaningful and positive learning experiences, which stretch and challenge them, is *mostly* dependent on the actions of schools and teachers.

Task 2.2   Focuses of causation

Using the table below, review your understanding of the three proposed focuses of causation of disability, namely individual differences (medical models), environmental demands (social models) and interaction analyses. You should consider these in relation to developing your understanding of the terms and implications for your practice.

The revised *Code of Practice* (DfE/DoH 2015) asks for schools to look within existing provision (SEN Supports), rather than regularly seek external advice and support as a means of addressing individual children's needs. Therefore, in order to respond to the needs of children with SEND at a more localised level, teachers need as part of their professional development to be given

	Interpretation of what each focus of causation stands for	Implications for your practice
Individual differences (medical models)		
Environmental demands (social models)		
Interactional analyses (combination of the two)		

opportunities to examine the impact of school cultures and pedagogical practices on either enabling or restricting inclusive education. This in part is being addressed through the Teachers' Standards (DfE 2013a) in which trainee teachers are required to have high expectations of all pupils, and adapt teaching to respond to the strengths and needs of all pupils. As a result, teachers are now required to think in many different ways about how their teaching approaches can enhance or deny access to an inclusive education for children with SEND.

Contradictions in attempts to plan for inclusive practice

In deducing how education systems in schools respond to diversity, Artiles (1998) suggests there is a 'dilemma of difference' within which fundamental mass education systems are established to deliver all students an 'education'. Mass education has, for instance, basic features of a common core of skills and knowledge, delivered in broadly equivalent circumstances, in schools with similar levels of training and pedagogies, which do not vary significantly from school to school, even in the context of the increasing 'academyisation' of schools.

However, if education is to fulfil the diversity it demands, Artiles (1998) suggests this can only be achieved by acting at individual pupil levels, which recognise children are different from each other. Pertinent to this is the need to construct and engage learning strategies that recognise different interests, aptitudes and expectations. This dilemma and tension brings with it difficulties in planning an appropriate education for children with SEND:

> If children identified as having a disability (needing special education) are offered the same learning experiences as other children, they are likely to be denied the opportunity to have learning experiences relevant to their individual needs. If children identified as having a disability (needing special education) are NOT offered the same learning experiences as other children, then they are likely to be treated as a separate and lower status group
> (Norwich 2008: 111–112)

This dilemma is entrenched in the development of educational policy in SEND over many years. The 1944 Education Act (DoE 1944) formalised a common education structure, in which all children were placed into different forms of schooling. The 1970s then involved increasing exploration of how far all children could be included within the same school, and in the 1980s the NC emerged, along with an exploration of mixed ability classes and concepts of differentiation. These developments were rooted in the concepts of 'equal access' and 'equal opportunities'. However, it is important to note, as Maher (2010) did, that equal access to opportunities does not mean that those opportunities will be inclusive. For instance, people with SEND may share the same learning space and receive the same teaching as pupils without SEND, but that does not always equate to their individual learning needs being met. Nonetheless, in the late 1990s and early part of the twenty-first century, and as a consequence of this evolving provision, Dyson and Millward suggest 'it is more helpful to think of inclusion as an outcome of actions within a school rather than as an inherent characteristic of the school' (Dyson and Millward 2000: 170).

Thus the measure of the extent to which inclusion is demonstrated in practice comes through the observation and charting of 'real life' case studies of children engaged in inclusive schools (see Coates and Vickerman 2009). As a result, teachers of the future need to be equipped with the knowledge, understanding, and strategies to enable inclusion to become a reality, and to be enabled to demonstrate this in outcomes that indicate positive and meaningful experiences for children with SEND. The place and time to gain the appropriate knowledge, skills and experiences is said to be during ITT (Maher et al. 2017; Morley et al. 2017).

Dilemmatic resolutions

Inclusive, and SEND, provision has been subject to 'a succession of dilemmatic resolutions' (Dyson and Millward 2000: 173), which have changed and emerged over many years. In addition, factors such as the introduction of the NC, OFSTED inspection and development of the *Code of Practice* (DfE/DoH, 2015) have signalled an ever-increasing scrutiny and control by Government on many issues of provision within schools. This brings with it a pressure between the espoused policy of schools, and policies pursued nationally by government and statutory agencies. Consequently, joined-up and collaborative approaches to inclusive education are essential if they are to become a reality for children with SEND. To some extent, in agencies such as OFSTED, with dual roles of inspection of ITT and school-based provision, this does give a better appreciation of what the issues and needs of the future are.

In the post-war years the education of children was largely by groupings of ability, in which 'streaming' was very much the order of the day as a means of integrating all pupils into mainstream contexts. Tansley and Guildford (1960) argue this was with the intention of not segregating people, but providing specialist provision through what at the time were referred to as 'remedial classes'. However, authors such as Carroll (1972), Collins (1972), and Galloway and Goodwin (1979), criticised this provision for its segregatory and stigmatising nature, and consequently streaming was seen as limiting the life opportunities to which children with special needs had access. This led to experiments with remedial work, and a shift in attention to 'whole class approaches' to teaching all pupils. This movement in thinking resulted in an emergence of 'whole school approaches' (Clark et al. 1995b), through which teachers would look to accommodate needs within the classroom, rather than through separate (remedial) classrooms and special needs teachers. This necessitated a change in curriculum pedagogy, in which 'ordinary' classes became fully accessible, with additional teacher support, and the role of the remedial teacher began to develop into one of a special educational needs co-ordinator (SENCO) (see Chapter 7). As a result, teachers of the future need to be given the necessary support and training within their ITT, and continuing professional development (CPD) to reflect upon the impact that their pedagogical practices can have in contributing to either positive or negative learning experiences. In addition, as part of their training, teachers need to know how to work collaboratively in order to provide a holistic approach to a child with SEND involving parents, support workers, health care professionals and the like, as laid out in the *Code of Practice* (DfE/DoH 2015).

Liberal principles and interchangeable terminology

In moving towards a more integrated structure of SEND provision, Clark et al. (1995b) suggest educational developments have been driven through relatively liberal principles. Whilst these principles have been contested, the history and development of special needs education in the UK are in tune with what we now term 'inclusion' (Dyson 1999). Consequently, the education system has been influenced through moderate principles of equity, valuing pupils' individual rights to participate, curricula learning experiences, and recognition that education and its goals are the same for all children (Warnock Report, DES 1978).

The key challenge for educationalists, though, is how this is interpreted in practice and provision for children with SEND within inclusive environments. Additionally, in relation to ITT providers, the challenge is to be able to equip teachers of the future with the necessary skills to respond to the requirements of the inclusion movement.

Lloyd (2000: 135) suggests:

> rather than developing inclusive approaches to practice in mainstream education, the integration of pupils with SEN has served to perpetuate and reinforce segregated practices, placing the impetus for change on the pupil.

Many factors have contributed to this viewpoint, which have mainly arisen out of 'fundamental misunderstanding and confusion about the concepts of integration and inclusion, and indeed the term SEN itself' (Lloyd 2000: 111). Dyson (2001), for example, argues there is a lack of consensus on what constitutes an equal education, failure to recognise all children's rights to learn, lack of how to identify SEND, and the resistance of practitioners to change. As a consequence, there is a need for significant debate and common ground to be established on what the related terms mean in policy and practice (Farrell 1998; Dyson 2001; Dyson and Millward 2000). Accordingly, Maher (2016) argues that it is not uncommon for policy makers, academics, researchers, school leaders, and teachers to use terms like mainstreaming, integration, and inclusion interchangeably as if they are synonymous. In this respect, it is important that there is some consensus among key stakeholders about what inclusion does, can and should involve to ensure that they have the same vision and are working towards providing the same learning experiences.

Within the UK, 'SEN' was introduced as a legally defined term in the Education Act 1981 (DES 1981) and 'refers to children's learning needs in school . . . is legally defined and this legal definition is used to decide whether particular children are eligible for special educational services' (Fredrickson and Cline 2002: 34).

In contrast, 'special needs' is not legally defined, and refers to needs experienced by pupils from most of the school population (i.e. homeless children, English as an additional language (EAL) pupils, and those from unstable family environments). As a consequence, the terms 'SEN' and 'special needs' are often used interchangeably (Dyson 2001; Ainscow et al. 1999) and this can 'causes unhelpful confusion since individuals from groups who have special needs may or may not have SEN' (Fredrickson and Cline 2002: 34).

Educational 'integration' is said to involve pupils with SEND acceding to dominant culture by espousing the established arrangements of education that are planned for those without SEND (Maher 2017). Here, there is an unsaid expectation that pupils with SEND should 'fit into' what is planned and delivered to the class (Fredrickson and Cline 2002). Consideration may be given to the needs of the pupil, but this often results in minor modifications being made to established learning activities. In contrast, inclusion is concerned with the introduction of more radical changes through which schools restructure themselves in order to embrace all children. Thus integration involves a process of assimilating an individual into existing structures, whilst inclusion is more concerned with accommodation, where the onus is on the school to change (Dyson 2001; Dyson and Millward 2000).

There is an obvious need for further clarification about inclusion at all levels from government policy through to professional practice with teachers. For example, at the policy level there is a need to be clear about what the terms mean in order to set clear expectations and resource inclusion effectively. At the professional opinion and practice (ITT provider) level trainee teachers need to be equipped with a full appreciation of the history, context, and interpretation of terminology. If this is successfully achieved through delivery in schools by PE teachers, there is a greater likelihood of inclusion becoming a reality for children with SEND.

Interpretations of inclusion

Concepts of inclusion have been subject to extensive debate in terms of their meaning and interpretation related to SEND. Ballard, a New Zealand scholar, noted, for example:

Inclusive education means education that is non-discriminatory in terms of disability, culture, gender or other aspects of students or staff that are assigned significance by a society. It involves all students in a community, with no exceptions and irrespective of their intellectual, physical, sensory or other differences, having equal rights to access the culturally valued curriculum of their society as full-time valued members of age-appropriate mainstream classes. Inclusion emphasises diversity over assimilation, striving to avoid the colonisation of minority experiences by dominant modes of thought and action.

(Ballard 1997: 244–245)

According to authors such as Dyson and Millward (2000), this definition is highly content specific and refers more to aspects of cultural diversity, rather than special needs education. They argue that the 1994 Salamanca Statement's interpretation of inclusion refers predominantly to finding basic forms of education for marginalised street children, working children, and those living in remote areas. In contrast, Dyson and Millward (2000) suggest inclusion within the UK has stronger links to its emergence through the work of Skrtic (1991, 1995) and Fuchs and Fuchs (1994), in which the American notion of inclusion grew out of a different social policy history based on civil rights, with particular reference to race, before the philosophy was transferred to the education of children with SEND. Booth et al. suggest:

Inclusion is a set of never ending processes. It involves the specification of the direction of change. It is relevant to any school however inclusive or exclusive its current cultures, policies and practices. It requires schools to engage in a critical examination of what can be done to increase the learning and participation of the diversity of students within the school locality.

(Booth et al. 2000: 12)

As a consequence, Daniels and Garner (1999) argue that, whilst it is important to recognise that inclusion can have global agreement, it is vital that inclusion is specifically interpreted within each national system. The development of inclusion and SEND within the UK should be considered therefore in terms of its particular history, culture and politics of its specific emerging system. As a consequence, it is 'dangerous to see the recent adoption of the inclusion agenda by the UK Government as a straightforward alignment with a policy direction that is both globally understood and relatively straightforward' (Dyson and Millward 2000: 4). As a result, the relationship between inclusion and SEND needs to be specifically aligned to the UK education system and Government provision in order to fully appreciate its underlying philosophies and practices.

Task 2.3   Terminology

Review your understanding of the distinctions between the terms SEND, special needs, integration and inclusion. How do you think having a clearer understanding and appreciation of these terms will help you in your practice of ensuring children with SEND gain positive PE experiences?

Changing school approaches: the shift from integration to inclusion

The difference between integration and inclusion is that the former applies to ways of supporting students with special needs in essentially unchanged mainstream schools. However, the latter refers to a radical restructuring of schools in order that they are inherently capable of educating all students within their communities (Corbett and Slee 2000). However, Dyson and Millward (2000) argue that this interpretation is too simplistic to apply to the UK system, in a background of longstanding expectations of mainstream schools to educate children with SEND. As a result, these expectations have involved the exploration of 'whole school approaches', in which teachers were required to consider 'fundamental changes in practice and organisation' (Dyson and Millward 2000: 8). This exploration has led to the dissolving of boundaries between special and mainstream education, as well as categories of special and ordinary children: 'and whole school response will essentially be a response to meeting the individual needs of children' (Dessent 1987: 121).

In examining the concept of 'whole school approaches', the emergence of the NC (2000) (QCA 1999a) added impetus to this shift, with its emphasis through the Statutory Inclusion Statement on setting suitable learning challenges, responding to individual diversity and differentiating assessment. These principles remained largely intact, although the wording has changed slightly, in the NC 2014 (DfE 2014a). Nonetheless, in the years following the introduction of the NC 2000, a number of schools were 'moving "beyond the whole school approach" in this sense towards what we chose to call "innovatory practice" in schools' approaches to special needs' (Dyson and Millward 2000: 10).

Thus according to Dyson and Millward (2000) school provision centred upon conceptualising approaches in terms of responses to student diversity as a whole, rather than simply a response to special needs; merging of special needs infrastructures within the mainstream; promoting differentiation through transformation of the curriculum and pedagogy; and redefining the role of SENCOs (Maher and Vickerman 2018; Dyson and Millward 2000).

The development of inclusive practices has seen some schools pushing back the boundaries of whole school approaches and exploring even further methods of enhancing teaching and learning for all pupils. This led Dyson and Millward (2000) to note that in some schools:

> quite dramatic transformations were evident – schools which disman-
> tled their special needs departments, abandoned all forms of segregated
> provision, reinvented their SENCOs as teaching and learning co-ordinators,
> embarked on intensive programmes of staff development, set up quality assur-
> ance programmes to enhance teaching and learning across the school and
> invested heavily in resource based learning in order to create flexible
> learning environments across the school.
>
> (Dyson and Millward 2000: 11)

> The inclusiveness of English schools has to be defined therefore not
> simply in terms of which students they educate, but in terms of how
> they educate them.
>
> (Dyson and Millward 2000: 11)

Consequently, inclusion is not about the mere presence of children with SEND, it has to lead to participation, be guided by notions of equity, and a fundamental recognition that the school system needs to adapt to meet the individual learning needs of the pupils it serves. In order to examine these changes in emphasis, Clark et al. (1995a) advocated that the practicality of inclusion, as well as the theoretical frameworks that underpin it, must be fully considered in order to arrive at a comprehensive appreciation of all the key issues of provision. This position is to some extent still reflected in 5(4) of the Teachers' Standards (DfE 2013a: 1), which states that teachers must

> have a clear understanding of the needs of all pupils, including those with
> special educational needs; those of high ability; those with English as an
> additional language; those with disabilities; and be able to use and evalu-
> ate distinctive teaching approaches to engage and support them.

Moving towards an understanding of inclusion

It is recognised that in recent years (along with many other aspects of SEND terminology) we have become used to the terms inclusion, inclusive education and inclusive schools being used interchangeably (Maher 2017; Vickerman 2007). In attempting to unpack the similarities and differences, it is rele-vant to note that within this chapter the complexities of inclusion need to be considered within a context that reflects government and statutory agencies, professional opinion and practice (teaching pedagogy), and consumer levels of classroom practice involving curriculum structure, experiences, and out-comes. Thus Clark et al.'s (1995a, 1997) view of interpretation of theoretical and practical contexts is still of particular relevance, and in considering this approach, Lipsky and Gartner suggest that 'while there is no single educational model or approach, inclusive schools tend to share similar characteristics and beliefs' (Lipsky and Gartner 1999: 17).

For example:

- **school-wide approaches** — in which the philosophy and practice of inclusive education is accepted by all the stakeholders;
- **all children learn together** — reflecting a continuum of learning needs within contexts of 'whole school approaches';
- **a sense of 'community' within schools** — through which children and teachers are valued (in addition, trainee teachers are required to demonstrate evidence of the promotion of positive values within the 02/02 (TTA 2002) 'Professional Standards Framework' (TTA 2002));
- **services based on need, rather than category** — recognising and responding to individual need as a starting point for supporting inclusive practice;
- **extensive teacher collaboration** — involving recognition of multiagency working, and thus linking with the desire of the DfES *Schools Achieving Success* (2001a) publication to promote collaborative working;
- **curriculum adaptation** — through which inclusion provides adaptations to enable all pupils to benefit from a common school curriculum;
- **enhanced instructional strategies** — encouraged and developed within ITT and continuing professional development (CPD), then facilitated in practice by teachers in schools;
- **standards and outcomes** — linked and drawn from those expected of children in general.

Whilst Lipsky and Gartner's (1999) list helps to identify a number of important inclusive school factors, Dyson and Millward (2000) argue that it also poses many problems, with the belief that all stakeholders will accept a particular philosophy or set of inclusive practices. In reality these 'fly in the face of what we know about the complexity of school life' (Dyson and Millward 2000: 18). This contrasting view of the interrelationship of theory and practice is one of many offering schools guidance on how to become more inclusive and indicates the extent to which inclusive education is both complex and problematic to implement (Runswick-Cole 2011).

In attempting to draw perspectives together, Dyson (2001) argued that in order to understand what inclusion stands for in principle and practice, the detail of many authors' views is weak on underpinning theoretical frameworks, organisational structures and processes that lead to either inclusion or exclusion. Consequently, in order to arrive at a thorough appreciation of inclusion for children with SEND, there is a need to examine the combined strengths of 'theoretical' and 'applied' views on inclusive practice. In Dyson's view, this can best be achieved through a collective critique of two authors' work, namely 'Skrtic's theoretical models of inclusive practice' and 'Ainscow's examination of applied inclusive practice' in schools. Therefore, in order to arrive at a coherent view of the fundamental principles, processes and practices concerned with inclusion, by examining the work of Skrtic and Ainscow a clearer picture should begin to emerge.

Skrtic's adhocratic schools

Skrtic (1991) argues from a position of 'crisis in modern knowledge', and a loss of confidence in the state of special education understanding. He believes that in arriving at the inclusive standpoint, the profession has been subject to a range of sociological, philosophical and political critiques. From a sociological perspective, Skrtic suggests professionals operate in a manner that realises the interests of its members, within the context of the organisations in which they operate, and consequently impose their own constraints and imperatives to suit their, rather than children's, needs. In contrast, philosophical perspectives refer to a wide-ranging transformation in the way in which knowledge and certainty have come to be understood, and recognise there is not one paradigm through which knowledge is universally transferred. Skrtic indicates that interpretivist, radical humanist, and radical structuralist paradigms have challenged the previously dominant functionalist paradigm of the 1960s, and as a direct consequence there are now many competing theories on special education (Pijl et al. 1997; Clark et al. 1995a; Clark et al. 1997; Dyson 2001).

Skrtic's political critique recognises that, in the past, the profession has argued from a position of access to privileged knowledge. However, this knowledge and understanding is now subject to scrutiny and questioning by competing theories, resulting in a diminishment of the power that they exercise over other people. In addition, the emergence of agencies such as OFSTED and the TTA (now the Teaching Agency (TA)) contributed to the diminishing power base originally dominated solely by the teaching profession. In appreciation of the changing nature of inclusive education, Skrtic takes the view that special education is grounded in four assumptions:

- disabilities are pathological;
- differential diagnosis is objective and useful;
- special education is a rationally conceived and co-ordinated system of services that benefit diagnosed pupils;
- progress results from incremental technological improvement in diagnosis and instructional interventions.

(Skrtic 1995: 54)

The special education field cannot therefore be grounded in foundational knowledge, and this view complements the UK position in which many researchers (Tomlinson 1982, 1985; Oliver 1988, 1990; Barton 1998) have indicated that disability has been constructed in a manner that serves the purposes of the profession rather than the client, and is subject to a range of views and opinions. This supports the earlier views of Pring (1996) and UCET (1997a) who note that many agencies and individuals have a role to play in determining what the nature of education, standards in ITT, and the Government's drive for 'school improvement' should consist of.

As a consequence, Skrtic suggests that whilst radical theorists claim to have changed the nature of SEND and inclusive provision, they have not sufficiently challenged the bureaucratic configuration of schools and the convergent thinking of the professional culture in a sufficiently fundamental manner (Skrtic 1995). Thus, whilst there has been a call for the dismantling of separate special schools, the bureaucracy still establishes systems that do not sufficiently respond to diversity, and Skrtic (citing Mintzberg 1979, 1983) designates this as an 'adhocracy'.

In considering this 'adhocracy', Skrtic explains:

> The professional bureaucracy is non adaptable because it is premised on the principle of standardisation, which configures it as a performance organisation for perfecting standard (rather than flexible) programmes. An adhocracy is premised upon principles of innovation, rather than standardisation; as such, it is a problem-solving organisation configured to invent new programs. It is the organisational form that configures itself around work that is so ambiguous and uncertain that neither the programs nor the knowledge and skills for doing it are known.
>
> (Skrtic 1991: 182)

The adhocratic organisation has therefore many advantages in that, Skrtic argues, it encourages collaboration between professionals with different kinds of expertise; involves discursive coupling through which teams reflect upon practice; team approaches in which theory and practice are unified through informal communication; professional – political accountability and a community of common interests. As a result:

> A school configured in this way would see the diversity of its students not as a disruption to be minimised by 'pigeonholing' the students into existing or separate programmes, but as a problem to be solved through a collaborative commitment to innovation.
>
> (Dyson and Millward 2000: 25)

This supports the view of the TA, who see teaching as a reflective-based profession and therefore this needs to be encouraged and fostered with trainee teachers as part of their ITT.

In summarising the adhocracy, Dyson and Millward (2000) suggest that Skrtic's views 'ultimately are philosophical rather than empirical. In particular, they are grounded in the theory of knowledge rather than in studies of actual schools' (Dyson and Millward 2000: 27).

However, Skrtic argues that the empirical realties of schools are intentionally not addressed, in order that they do not interrupt the open and free flow of his thinking, rather than establish arguments around constraints of existing structures. Thus, it is for others to look to how the adhocratic models can be implemented structurally (official line) and delivered in practice (professional opinion and practice and impact on the consumers).

In response, Dyson and Millward (2000) cite the work of Ainscow, and his notion of 'the moving school' in which he documents 'good inclusive practice' in schools as an answer to the need to provide empirical substance to the inclusion debate. Consequently, Ainscow is concerned with documenting not only the good practice but also, more significantly, what, why and how it is deemed to be good inclusive practice. As a result, Ainscow's documented practice is grounded in wider circumstances of institutional development, professional development and special education.

Ainscow's documentation of inclusive school practice

Ainscow defines inclusion as:

> a process of increasing the participation of pupils in, and reducing their exclusion from, the cultures, curricula and communities of their local schools, not forgetting, of course, that education involves many processes that occur outside of schools.
>
> (Ainscow 1999: 218)

He suggests inclusion is often viewed as involving movement from special to mainstream contexts under a belief that once there they will be 'included'. Inclusion should, however, be considered 'as a never ending process, rather than a simple change of state, and as dependent on continuous pedagogical and organisational development within the mainstream' (Ainscow 1999: 218).

This view is of particular interest to Dyson and Millward (2000), as Ainscow links pedagogical development to teacher development, and then assimilates this to the organisational development of schools. This standpoint is at the centre of Ainscow's model of inclusive practice in which he advocates a desire to move away from views of locating the problem with the child, and look to an examination of curriculum adaptation and modification (social model). Consequently, inadequacies of learning environments should be seen as generating the learning difficulty, rather than the individual characteristics (medical model) of the pupil (Ainscow 1994). In order to develop the theme of curricula, rather than pupil adaptation, Ainscow (1999) believes that schools must become 'moving schools', which are in a constant state of inclusive development and change in order to adapt to the individual needs of all its pupils. Schools should therefore be looking to develop their inclusive practice around a number of core areas, namely:

- effective leadership – incorporating a clear vision and strategy for making inclusive practice work;
- involvement of all staff, students and the community – so that all people understand their rights and responsibilities to respect and value diversity;
- commitment to collaborative planning – in which, through multiagency working, children with SEND receive a holistic approach to their education;
- attention to the benefits of enquiry and reflection – supporting teachers as reflective practitioners, constantly prepared to modify, adapt or radically change their teaching and learning approaches;
- policies for staff development that focus on classroom practice – through which all staff are offered opportunities for continuing professional development to enhance their knowledge and understanding.

The fundamental premise of inclusive school practice is designed therefore to support Ainscow's notion of a changing school, responding flexibly to the individual need of its pupils, rather than the other way around in which children have to adapt to fit pre-existing educational settings. As a result of the notions of constantly changing schools, Dyson and Millward (2000) argue that due to the empirical basis of Ainscow's views there is significant credence in supporting his models of inclusive practice in schools. Consequently, ITT needs to be constructed within a framework of creating reflective teachers who are responsive and adaptable to the individual needs of pupils that they serve in schools.

Common themes – an inclusive approach to teaching children with SEND

The work of Skrtic and Ainscow has made significant contributions toward articulated theoretical accounts of the relationship between principles and processes of inclusive practice and school organisation. Within this context, attempts have been made to identify 'common themes' that have emerged in schools with reference to inclusive principles and practices, whilst identifying potential threats to this movement. Thus, whilst classes and schools may be very different in their approaches, it is possible, according to Dyson and Millward (2000), to establish characteristics of a 'model of the inclusive school', which can then be used as a basis for all the key stakeholders to work towards the creation of inclusive schools. In reflecting on the work of Skrtic and Ainscow, inclusive schools can be characterised by:

- **effective leadership** – in which all people in positions of responsibility (whether that be at Government, ITT or school level) drive forward and disseminate the belief of inclusive practice;

- **clear vision** – in which all stakeholders work together to promote inclusive practice;
- **dismantling of structures and barriers** – through which agencies and individuals are prepared to review, modify and change policies and practices whether they be physical, ideological, attitudinal or financial barriers and constraints;
- **response to diversity** – in which difference is valued as an essential component of the make-up of schools and wider society;
- **senior management responsibility** – in which people in positions of responsibility ensure that the visions of inclusive practice become a reality;
- **reliance on in-class support** – in contrast to separate or segregated provision;
- **emphasis on the professional development of staff** – as the future of inclusive provision rests with the skills, expertise and determination of staff to make inclusive practice a reality for children with SEND.

Conclusion and future directions in inclusion for children with SEN

Dyson and Millward (2000) argue that through a combination of Ainscow's and Skrtic's inclusive models, and their own case studies of common themes lending empirical weight, an 'illuminating explanation' (Dyson and Millward 2000: 149) of the nature of inclusive education for children with SEND begins to emerge. Thus, in taking account of 'the multiple values' (Norwich 2002: 484) offered by the authors above, a clearer picture on the nature of training required to equip teachers of PE begins to emerge.

Task 2.4   Characteristics of inclusive schools

Review your understanding of the similarities and differences between Skirtic's adhocratic schools and Ainscow's documentation of inclusive practice and what you see as the implications for teaching children with SEND in PE. Once you have done this, use the table below to look at the common theme of inclusive practice and reflect upon what you understand by each aspect and its relationship to teaching children with SEND in PE.

In support of a clearer picture emerging on the nature of inclusive practice, Reynolds et al. (2000) note that two paradigms have dominated school changes, and consequently have assisted with the development of teaching and learning

Characteristics of inclusive schools	Your understanding of the aspect	Relationship to teaching children with SEN in PE
Effective leadership: all people in positions of responsibility drive forward the belief of inclusive practice		
Clear vision: all stakeholders work together to promote inclusive practice		
Dismantling of structures and barriers: agencies and individuals are prepared to review, modify and change policies and practices		
Response to diversity: difference is valued as an essential component of the make up of schools		
Senior management responsibility: people in positions of responsibility ensure visions of inclusive practice become a reality		
Reliance on in-class support: in contrast to separate or segregated provision		
Emphasis on the professional development of staff: future of inclusive provision rests with the skills, expertise and determination of staff		

approaches for children with SEND. The first is concerned with a 'top-down process', which is centrally designed, through which innovation and change is transmitted to schools. In contrast, the 'bottom-up process' involves building upon the professional development of teachers and involving them fully in the development of school improvement and inclusive practice.

Dyson and Millward (2000) state that educational progress is fraught with conflict, contest and compromise out of which may come policy positions that are far from coherent. In contexts of top-down and bottom-up change processes, therefore, and the nature of conflict, it is easy to appreciate why apparently well intentioned models of inclusion, integration or whole school approaches for children with SEND seem often to deliver less than they initially promise (Lloyd 2000; Croll and Moses 2000). This conflicting picture:

> has illuminated the way in which such policies, both in formation and in practice, are shaped by, inter alia, ambiguous and contradictory national imperatives, interacting with the competing interests of head teachers, parents and others with a vested interest in the nature of that provision.
>
> (Dyson and Millward 2000: 157)

School improvement, and inclusive theories and practices, become ever more complex and problematic to disentangle (Rouse and Florian 1997; Vincent et al. 1994; Vislie and Langfeldt 1996). As a result, Feiler and Gibson (1999) argue that within this background there are four potential threats to the inclusion movement, which need to be addressed as a matter of urgency prior to any further developments in relation to the education of children with SEND, which are:

- a lack of consistency in the definition and understanding of inclusion;
- a lack of empirical data;
- notions of internal exclusion (i.e. streaming or grouping);
- a tendency to describe individual needs in a manner that implies the problem resides with the child, rather than the school structure.

In reflecting upon these four threats, the future development of special needs education needs to move towards a coherent framework within which government policy is reflected, delivered, and implemented within a structure that ensures all agencies and individuals are clear about what the vision of inclusive schooling involves. In summary, with regard to future visions, Dyson succinctly makes the following statements, which act as a point for further reflection: 'Special needs education so patently has a past and that past – like the present – is highly fluid and even turbulent' (Dyson 2001: 24). In coming to terms with the future:

> It is my contention that the inherent instability of the present means that it is incumbent on us to look carefully at what the future might hold. Even as the 'new' resolution of 'inclusion' struggles to establish its hegemony, we should, I believe, try to understand how it will ultimately fragment and what possibilities might open up for alternative resolutions.
> (Dyson 2001: 27)

Chapter 3

Movement, learning and ranges of special educational needs and disabilities

Introduction

Children with SEND, like all children, need to experience physical movement, learning and development in a wide range of activities and environments as part of their education. The rationale for supporting the development of children's movement patterns is twofold: first for their own physical development, and second it can be seen as an essential aspect of their social, emotional, intellectual and cognitive development.

For children, physical activity and movement enhances fitness, fosters growth and development, and helps teach them about their world. As teachers of young children, we know that most children are innately physically active and that they learn as they move around their environment. Consequently, in observing children at break times, we often see them running, jumping, throwing, and playing in informal and unstructured settings.

However, in today's modern age of computers, concerns over child safety and longer working hours for parents, young people often find themselves involved in sedentary alternatives. Children, in short, spent a lot of time sitting or lying and less time moving (see Pearson et al. 2014). For example, children tend to ride in a car or bus to school, have less PE, watch more television, play more sedentary games, and do not have as much freedom to play outside on their own. Consequently, there is mounting evidence that even the youngest of children are becoming less physically active and more overweight and obese. This is contributing to an increased prevalence of childhood obesity and other risk factors. These concerns have resulted in the *Start Active, Stay Active* Report (DoH 2011), which provides guidelines on the frequency and type of physical activity required for children and adults to achieve health benefits. Interestingly, the report provides guidance for early years (under 5) children, something that has never been done before in UK public health guidelines. When discussing children and young people aged 5–18, the report suggests:

> During this period, children and young people establish behaviour patterns that have important implications for their immediate and long-term

health and well-being. Among the myriad social, emotional and institutional transitions that take place are reductions in habitual levels of physical activity and increased participation in certain sedentary behaviours; these changes have important public health implications.

(DoH 2011: 26)

The guidelines for children and young people are:

- all children and young people should engage in moderate to vigorous intensity physical activity for at least 60 minutes and up to several hours every day;
- vigorous intensity activities, including those that strengthen muscle and bone, should be incorporated at least three days a week;
- all children and young people should minimise the amount of time spent being sedentary (sitting) for extended periods.

(DoH 2011: 26)

The guidelines are for all children and young people, regardless of the social-economic status, race or gender. However, when it comes to children with SEND, the Department for Health (2011: 26) suggest that the guidance 'can be applied to disabled children and young people, emphasising that they need to be adjusted for each individual based on that person's exercise capacity and any special health issues or risks'.

Whilst all of the issues and concerns raised with regard to sedentary physical activity are equally applied to children with SEND, what is often the case is that as a consequence of their disabilities this can be compounded even further and immobility for whatever reasons can lead to increased weight, therefore making movement progressively harder. This chapter sets out to examine the fundamental principles of learning and movement before proceeding to an overview of the range of SEND that teachers are likely to be presented with in school. As with other chapters, the purpose of providing detailed overviews of children with SEND is in order for teachers to review existing practices and be fully prepared to modify and adapt teaching and learning activities to maximise opportunities for positive PE experiences.

Learning to move, moving to learn

There is considerable awareness of the contribution that PE lessons have on the physical, social, emotional and intellectual development of all children. However, PE has an even greater role to play in the overall growth and development of the vast majority of pupils with SEND. The relevance and importance of learning through physical activity cannot be overstated. In relation to PE, a SEND can be attributed to any child who has a movement difficulty, which in reality involves a broad range of pupils. However, in addition to this rather generalised statement there are many groups of children who can easily be recognised as having a SEND in PE. These include:

- sensory impairments (both visual and auditory);
- locomotion and other movement problems;
- severe or moderate learning difficulties;
- medical conditions such as diabetes, epilepsy or asthma;
- emotional and behavioural disorders;
- profound and multiple learning difficulties.

Many of these conditions can lead to a lack of confidence in body management, which in turn leads to difficulties in gaining positive experiences in PE and this is where the teacher is vital to the process of ensuring children with SEND do not feel disadvantaged. Furthermore, it is important that PE for children with SEND is not seen purely in a physical light, as many activities present additional opportunities to develop social skills that can lead to a free and independent life in a context that is relevant, real, pleasurable, and creative. An exciting PE programme can stimulate and motivate pupils who in turn are less likely to become frustrated or emotionally disturbed, and consequently children with SEND should be given every opportunity and encouraged to use these opportunities to the best of their ability.

The aims of PE for pupils with SEND are no different from those of any other child, in that they are entitled to a broad, balanced, progressive, differentiated, and relevant programme of activities. Clearly, some children will have greater difficulties than others in terms of active participation, but it is important that provision be made for their inclusion alongside their peers. It is also important to note that, should it be necessary for an activity or equipment to be modified or substituted, it maintains its educational integrity. Pupils with SEND by their very nature are individuals who possess a wide range of personal and specific needs that have enormous complexity and diversity. To offer a comprehensive programme in PE will present considerable challenges for teachers and schools and the task therefore lies in the identification of individual needs and provision of a range of activities to satisfy these needs. The skills learnt and experiences shared will support them and carry them forward into adult life and assist them towards an active and worthwhile role within the community. The teacher's reward is to see each pupil develop and attain their full potential.

What are movement patterns and motor development?

Any movement pattern can be described as a definite arrangement of muscle actions that are required to achieve a desired outcome. For example, throwing a ball, turning around or jumping in the air are all distinctive movement patterns. Movement patterns can be likened to general templates that then become the basis for a number of specific skills such as those used in gymnastics, dance or games activities. Thus, an underarm throw can be described as a movement pattern, whilst a bowl in rounders or a pass in netball can be seen as specific skills that develop from it. Furthermore, a turn of the whole body is seen as a movement pattern whilst a spin in dance or turn in gymnastics are referred to as specific skills that develop from it.

It is vital for all children that basic movement patterns are established before progression to specialised skill development. Most movement patterns become established during the early years of child development provided they have had sufficient stimulus and opportunity to utilise them. Whilst some children may need more encouragement than others to practise and apply them in different situations, usually by the age of around seven most children will have sound templates of movement patterns. However, for some children with SEND this achievement may take much longer and require significant intervention, adaptation, and support.

The establishment of sound basic movement patterns allows children to progress by building upon these templates and combining and refining them to specific situations and developing specialist skills. PE offers an opportunity to support this development, particularly in primary school in the Foundation and Key Stage One phases. This supports the requirement of the PE NC 2014, which states that: 'Pupils should develop fundamental movement skills, become increasingly competent and confident and access a broad range of opportunities to extend their agility, balance and coordination, individually and with others' (DfE, 2014d: 2). These can be seen as the foundations of all future physical learning and PE teachers in these early stages should focus more on learning generalised movement patterns rather than specific skill development, which can be focused upon at a later stage.

Supporting children to develop and learn motor skills

The dual processes of learning and development are responsible for much of what we observe in children's skill. These are stimulated by qualities such as motivation and persistence, although development and learning are central to what a child offers and receives in the PE setting. These concepts, although different, are also difficult to separate, with developments being a combination of maturation and the interrelationship with everyday experiences and learning. Clearly, these will be different according to the phase of development a child is at, although by teachers examining these processes it helps to provide a better foundation and understanding of children's functioning which in turn will contribute towards ensuring they have positive PE experiences.

Although there are no distinctive stages in a child's motor development, there are global phases the child passes through from birth to maturity. As a result, it is important to consider these phases from birth because many children with SEND will show movement characteristics of children who are much younger. Whilst age in years and months is not a totally accurate guide to development because of individual differences, it does offer some comparability to make judgements about children and SEND. This is particularly true with children with SEND whose developmental progress can vary dramatically from those who are in typical ranges, and may continue to remain delayed even in later childhood.

From birth to two years of age

During this period, children develop rapidly and acquire three basic skills of **locomotion, posture**, and **manipulation.** Posture can be seen as the precursor to locomotion and involves the control of various parts of the body, such as the head and trunk, whilst lying and sitting prior to eventual progression to an upright stance. In some children with SEND who have profound and/ or multiple learning difficulties, these developmental progressions may provide the basis for targets and learning activities during PE lessons. One of the key milestones in any child's development is progression to upright locomotion, which typically occurs around one year of age but varies significantly with children with SEND. From a child's first steps they use this newfound skill in a number of environmental contexts leading to complex locomotor activities that we seek to present and develop in our PE lessons. Again, the variations of upright locomotion usually found in the first two years of life can provide opportunities for children of all ages. Manipulation progresses steadily in the first two years, with reaching becoming more accurate and grasping changing from crude palmed responses to delicate pincer grips involving the thumb and first finger. In PE, reaching for and grasping objects of different sizes, shapes, weights, colours, and textures can provide the foundation stones for many activities. Therefore, if necessary, progression can be used by PE teachers to present movement situations to children in their lessons that accommodate the particular stage of development that they are at.

Task 3.1   Defining key terms

Reflect on your understanding of the terms locomotion, posture, and manipulation and consider their relationship to PE and the type of activities you can employ to support and enhance their development.

From age two through to seven years of age

During this period, children develop all the basic locomotor skills alongside self-help skills. For example, by the age of six or seven most children can run, jump, hop, skip, throw, climb, catch, kick, stride out, dress, wash, produce recognisable letters and shapes, and perform everyday manipulation skills. Whilst children may not be able to do all of these to a highly accomplished level, most will be able to execute them in a rudimentary fashion. However, some children with SEND will either be delayed or have great difficulty in executing these and this may again be a fundamental focus for work and support within PE lessons.

When a child with SEND has difficulty with these tasks it can occur for a variety of reasons. For example, it may be due to a child not experiencing the full range of everyday daily living experiences that are normally associated with standard child development. If this is the case, the child may enter pre-school or school without the necessary skills, but then may quickly gain them with exposure to the right type of activities within PE lessons. It is desirable for children at this stage of development to have a vocabulary and motor skills vocabulary that allow them to be more flexible and utilise these in a variety of situations rather than go down a route of exacting specific and highly defined tasks. However, whilst some children will progress rapidly once they enter school, others (especially those with SEND) will continue to pose challenges for teachers.

Therefore, any PE or movement-based programme should incorporate a diverse range of skills rather than seek depth, in order to provide the basis for more specific skills that will appear later. It is also during this period of development that natural progression of locomotor skills takes place. For example, in relation to jumping the first jump is often a step down from one foot to the other, followed by a two-foot take-off from the ground. A two-foot standing long jump follows this, with alterations to arm and body positions, before mature jumping skills are perfected. It is also worth noting that jumping occurs before hopping, which in turn starts before skipping.

Differences between boys and girls are not significant at these phases, although boys tend to be superior in ball skills whilst girls are superior at rhythmic co-ordination such as hopping and skipping tasks. Towards the end of this phase, studies have found greater incidence of clumsiness in boys than in girls, which is worth noticing and being ready for as part of the planning process for PE lessons.

Age seven years through to puberty

It is at this phase of motor development that children do not acquire new fundamental skills. Rather, what they are doing is going through a process of refining, honing, and elaborating upon the skills they have already gained and now begin to adapt them to new situations, make them more elegant, use them in a variety of contexts, and respond to changing environmental demands. Consequently, children who were competent at controlling movements now progress to situations where they need to become competent with others rather than just themselves.

By the age of seven they have control of their own bodies but are generally not good at responding and reacting to environmental demands. Children before age seven do not have spontaneous responses to situations that demand that they respond to moving environments, such as running to strike a moving ball. It is at this stage where individual differences become more noticeable and particularly where distinctions can become significant and more apparent in children with SEND alongside their age-peers.

The natural development in children has significant implications for PE, especially at the primary phase when tasks are presented in varying contexts with different people and social groupings. Therefore, it is critical that PE activities are structured in a manner that allows children to make spatial and temporal decisions often at speed. Children from seven through to puberty are developing perceptually and cognitively, and development in these carries over into the motor domain. Children show great expectation, for example in anticipation and predictive skills that are crucial to playing games activities, whilst additionally requiring responses to others in fast- moving environments.

In relation to children with SEND, it can be considered even more important because many of their needs are much more complex and involve other interacting areas in addition to motor skills. For example, perceptual and cognitive systems may not be as developed and situations that involve prediction and anticipation may need to be simplified. It is here that gender differences can become present, whereby boys tend to continue to be proficient at ball skills and are up to a year ahead in running, speed and jumping distances. In contrast, girls continue to show superior ability in rhythmic and co-ordinated activities whilst showing lower incidences of motor difficulties and delay.

From puberty through to adulthood

This phase brings great physical changes in a person's capacity, with children becoming bigger, stronger, and having greater physical capability. It is also at this stage that children begin to choose which activities to take part in as part of school sport or physical activity and leisure outside of school. It is worth noting here, though, that increases in strength are often compensated for by a lack of skill at this stage so it is vital for children to be presented with skilful learning situations in PE that continue to enable them to participate recreationally as well as part of the PE curriculum. There is also significant variability in the onset of puberty, which can start as young as nine in some girls and be as late as 15 in some boys. Boys tend to go through puberty for a longer period of time and change occurs at greater intensities. Consequently, boys who are at the post-puberty stage tend to be as a group better at power, strength, and endurance activities. However, on tasks that require pure skilled movements there is no significant gender difference.

These differences enable children with SEND opportunities to experience different types of activity depending on their specific needs. However, it is necessary to show some degree of caution in that children with severe learning difficulties may be going through puberty biologically, yet socially, emotionally, and cognitively may be functioning at a much lower level. This kind of developmental profile has significant implications and raises issues that require consideration in relation to the nature and manner within which tasks are presented in PE lessons.

The learning process in PE

When children attempt to learn a new task the first operation is the need to **understand the skill**, with teachers simultaneously knowing how to get children to develop the skill in the first instance and how to get them to understand what is demanded of them and the resources they need to meet that demand. This is a critical aspect of the learning process and one that is sometimes overlooked. As a result, if teachers do overlook this part, the rest of the learning process (especially in relation to SEND) cannot be fully successful. Consequently, during this part of the learning process it is vital that teachers offer demonstrations, instructions, and explanations that bring clarity to the situations that are being presented to them.

The second aspect of the learning process involves **acquiring and refining skills**, whereby the child knows what to do and is now involved in the actual physical process of learning and development. During this aspect of learning teachers need to point out what is right and help with aspects that need refinement and correction. As a teacher, observational skills are vital here in order to provide immediate and constructive feedback to children. The third part is **automatising these skills,** where the child becomes quite competent and performs without paying much attention to it. Another aspect that permeates across all stages is **generalising the skill,** involving children using the skills learned so far to help them with a new skill that has been presented to them. Whilst these skills will overlap with each other it is not useful to try to make definitive distinctions at this stage, whilst observational skills in teachers are again vital here.

In PE lessons teachers are involved in a series of activities that stimulate the learning process, which involve:

- providing instructions and explanations;
- giving demonstrations;
- providing appropriate practices and giving timely feedback.

Task 3.2   The four elements of the learning process

Use the table below to reflect on four elements of the learning process in PE. You should consider your understanding of each of the terms and its relationship to PE, whilst additionally considering any implications for teaching children with SEND.

Whilst the above is not the total sum of the teaching process, they do take a significant proportion of a teacher's time. The issue for you as a teacher becomes one of how the teaching activities change through the different learning phases that children pass through. Whilst absolute protocols cannot be provided, there are guidelines to consider and reflect upon as part of your planning of PE lessons. For example, when a child is first learning a new skill, instructions need to be short and very clear, with the objective of getting the child into the task as quickly as possible. Here, feedback is essential and needs to be short and explicit, with practice engaging children in simple activities.

As the child acquires and refines the skill, instructions and feedback can become more detailed; although practice needs to focus on one or two aspects, it can become more varied. In children with SEND it may be necessary to spend longer on certain aspects of tasks. For example, children with learning difficulties often have problems getting into the task. Once they are doing it they are fine, but getting to that point can be problematic for them and for you as a teacher, and can test your ingenuity, flexibility and adaptation and modification skills. As a result, more time may need to be spent in ensuring a child with SEND understands what is required, and this may involve extensive elaboration and further explanation.

The ranges of SEND

The first point to make in any discussion on ranges of SEND is that not all children will have difficulties in PE lessons. For example, a child with emotional and behavioural difficulties could excel in gymnastics or a child with learning difficulties may be an excellent swimmer. Consequently, we should

Aspect of the learning process	Your interpretation and its relationship to PE	Considerations related to children with SEND
Understanding the skill		
Acquiring and refining the skill		
Automatising the skill		
Generalising the skill		

not assume that SEND equals difficulty. However, pupils with SEND are going to pose challenges for you as the teacher and this is where having an open mind, high expectations, and a willingness to adapt your practices are critical to successful PE experiences. This part of the chapter will now provide you with a range of characteristics of children with SEND, but it is important to stress this is not a definitive list, and it is essential that you continue to recognise and value the uniqueness of each child. Consequently, developing strategies for consultation and flexibility should remain a constant focus for your practice. Thus, the following overview on ranges of SEND should merely act as a starting point for your reflection, and not an end point.

The adaptation of practices and/or lack of access to PE for a child with SEND are particularly well reinforced in the statement by Fredrickson and Cline (2002: 40) who suggest, 'at one extreme then, the environmentally focused approach holds that there are no students with learning difficulties, only adults with teaching difficulties'. Consequently, the requirement to modify and adapt practices (reinforced through the PE NC 2014 and Teachers' Standards) suggests that any barriers or lack of success in many aspects will come down to you as the teacher and not generally be any fault of the child's. As a result, it is essential that we start from the premise that all children can learn and develop if the right opportunities are provided for them.

What you need to do as the teacher is examine the interrelated dynamics of the teacher, the environment, and the individual needs of the child, which can all be considered as essential ingredients in the success or lack of PE lessons for children with SEND. Thus, children have certain ranges of movement that need to be considered fully by the teacher in order to provide a successful outcome. What you need to do as the teacher is ensure that selection and breakdown of the task is appropriate in order to achieve a successful result. Finally, the environmental context can make or break the success of the child, which involves you, the teaching space, and the other pupils within the class.

Task 3.3   Three interacting variables of teaching and learning

Reflect on the ways in which the individual needs of children, the teaching environment and you as the teacher interact, and examine the strategies you would employ to ensure positive outcomes in PE for children with SEND.

It is often the case that children with SEND are classified according to the severity of their particular conditions. However, whilst this can initially appear to be logical, it is not the most useful or productive point from which to progress forward. For example, there are some children with severe conditions who only require minimal adaptations, whilst others with fewer and less complex needs require significant intervention. The other issue to note here relates to a requirement upon you to take a social model approach and consider what you need to do to fit your teaching and learning environment around the child, rather than the other way around. Consequently, the descriptions below illustrate some of the characteristics of children with SEND whilst still recognising that children with these conditions can have very different needs and responses to PE, movement and learning.

Children with specific movement difficulties

In any education, health and care (EHC) plan, or in earlier stages of the *Code of Practice*, children with specific movement difficulties are recognised for their needs in the movement domain and usually have medical conditions that supplement these. It is important again to recognise that the potential for a positive outcome is great and you as the teacher need to establish high expectations, an open mind, and a commitment to modify and adapt practices as necessary.

Cerebral palsy covers a range of conditions that manifest themselves through poor motor control as a result of damage to the brain. Whilst children with cerebral palsy do not notably experience deterioration in their condition, changes do take place that make diagnosis a little unstable. The damage is usually early in childhood and the most significant impact is impairment of movement accompanied by other related difficulties. Many children with cerebral palsy may also have general learning, speech, and language difficulties. Cerebral palsy is classified in a number of ways, but teachers are most likely to see it described through the characteristics noted below. A child's cerebral palsy is usually referred to as mild, moderate or severe. However, this is not the total picture as children are also classified according to the location of their impairment. For example, we have terms like **quadriplegia** (all four limbs are affected), **hemiplegia** (one side involved, or one side involved more than the other), **diplegia** (legs only affected, or more so than the arms).

The third aspect of classification examines the types of movement that a child performs, which are commonly referred to as **spasticity**, involving muscle tone, build-up of tension and releasing movements. The often noticeable rigid tonus is not always present, and can vary according to emotional states and which part of the body is involved. Abnormal reflexes are typical of all types of cerebral palsy and in spasticity the child has great difficulty in breaking free of the movements imposed upon them by their reflexes. This is compounded through involuntary control by the increased hyperconicity, which in some cases can be so severe that it can fixate the limbs in a few typical postures. In addition, when working with children with cerebral palsy you are often likely to see what is referred to as a 'scissor gait', which is presented by flexion of the hip, knee, and ankle and rotation of the leg towards the midline, creating balance and locomotion difficulties.

The second major type of cerebral palsy is referred to as **athetosis**, which involves fluctuating muscle tone, often resulting in what looks like seemingly purposeless and uncontrollable movements; children may display writhing, squirming, and swiping movements. These fluctuations in muscle control can make it difficult for children to maintain a stable posture, and this is heightened by muscle spasms, flexion, and extension. The situation is often compounded further by athetoid and spastic movements that result in lack of head control, which can impact upon visual tracking activities in PE.

Ataxia is another form of cerebral palsy, and is characterised by postural instability and problems in balance and co-ordination, which show when children sit, walk, and stand. There is usually poor fixation of the head and trunk, and this promotes a stumbling gait whereby movements appear clumsy.

It is important to recognise that children with cerebral palsy can take part in PE, and play an active part in these lessons. The key to creating successful PE experiences for such children is in appreciating the issues and needs discussed above, and your response to the challenges they pose to your teaching and learning.

Spina bifida is part of a group of conditions in which formation of the neural tube is compromised. The higher the site of damage, the more disabling the condition. Prevalence has been estimated at between 1 and 3 per 1,000, and children have a range of abilities from those requiring a wheelchair to those who are ambulant. There may also be some difficulties with fine motor movements and perceptual difficulties, and some children may be incontinent, which requires management.

Muscular dystrophy is part of a subgroup of conditions caused by disorders of the neuromuscular system, and is characterised by wasting and progressive weakness of the muscles. It is different from the other conditions described above in that the physical condition deteriorates over time, although teaching and therapy can help to slow down the process. Children with muscular dystrophy will need careful monitoring, planning, and emotional support.

Children with **brittle bones** have a predisposition to bone fractures, caused by a lack of the protein collagen, which gives strength to bones and ligaments. This can be potentially hazardous, but through considered discussion with parents and medical staff they can still have positive PE experiences. Other conditions, such as cystic fibrosis, diabetes, asthma, epilepsy, and haemophilia also impact on children's movement. If you are interested in finding out more about the characteristics of such conditions, you can refer to the work of Winnick and Porretta (2017).

Children with general movement difficulties

Children who lack the movement skills necessary to function effectively in PE lessons, yet have no identifiable neurological disorder, are fairly common in schools. They tend to exhibit delayed performances with movement skills, which can generally be described as at functionally low levels. Terms used to describe these children have included clumsiness, clumsy child syndrome, and dyspraxia. However, the most recent and widely recognised term is Development Co-ordination Disorder (DCD). Children with DCD acquire the basic skills of sitting, standing and walking but these may be delayed, and they usually have difficulty in demonstrating the flexibility to adapt to changing environmental conditions. They can usually perform skills at rather rudimentary levels but are less skilled than their peers, often have difficulty using skills in context and their movement patterns look rather awkward. This can lead to a lack of participation in PE and other leisure and play activities.

PE is not the only subject in which DCD is present and poses challenges for children, as most aspects of the NC require a basic level of motor competence. For example, in studies by Sugden and Henderson (1994) children with DCD have been identified as having problems with activities such as pouring, weighing, cutting, drawing, and writing. They may also present with social, emotional, and behavioural problems due to the difficulties they have with their movement.

The incidence of DCD varies, but research tends to suggest that around 5 per cent of children aged 5 to 11 years of age may have DCD, which results in around one or two children per class requiring support. Most studies have found incidence of DCD to be higher in boys, with the condition not having any fixed boundaries or clear characteristics but with a clear expectation that teachers will be required to modify and adapt their PE lessons. Research has shown that DCD is a condition that children do not grow out of, and this has been exemplified in studies where children with poor motor skills at six years of age still exhibit movement difficulties when re-tested ten years later. However, those who do improve tend to have had specific PE programmes that have worked on supporting their specific movement needs. Consequently, if children with DCD are left to their own devices they generally do not improve, and this may go on to affect other aspects of their social, physical, emotional, and behavioural functioning both in and outside of school. On the other hand, children with DCD movement skills who undertake structured and specific intervention programmes that are managed in conjunction with occupational therapists, physiotherapists, and PE teachers have shown significant improvement.

Children with learning difficulties

There are groups of children in schools (whether mainstream or special) who are not recognised for their physical disabilities, nor are they classified as clumsy or having DCD, yet they still have generalised movement difficulties as part of their overall profile. These children are referred to in the UK as **children with learning difficulties**, and they are usually identified in relation to their functional needs and difficulties in school subjects. In other countries, IQ scores are used to group children along a continuum from mild through moderate to severe and profound, and in the USA these children are referred to as having an intellectual disability or intellectual developmental disorder. In the UK, we tend to group children through a range from mild to moderate, severe and profound, and in addition there are identifiable sub groups such as **Down syndrome**.

There is a higher incidence of motor difficulties among children who are classed as having moderate learning difficulties, and as the severity of learning increases so does the incidence of motor difficulties. However, it is important to stress that some children with moderate learning difficulties will have no motor difficulties and will perform well, and even excel, in PE. As a result, as stressed on many occasions previously, it is important to look at the individual needs of each child and consult with children, parents, and support workers rather than make generalisations. This will involve you having to reflect on learning activities such as task adaptation, breaking down of tasks into smaller components, and consideration of levels and degrees of feedback.

Children with sensory difficulties

Children with sensory difficulties in relation to being **blind** or **deaf** as a group also tend to have movement difficulties and will pose some challenges for teachers in PE lessons. For example, a child who has a visual impairment will find that this will impact upon their movement abilities, and you as a teacher will need to give consideration to the organisation of spatial information. In most children with visual difficulties vision is likely to be to some extent impaired rather than not present at all. This is where the need for teachers to consult with the individual child, parents, and support workers is critical to a successful and positive outcome in PE.

As children who have a visual impairment grow up, they tend to have difficulty with everyday tasks such as walking, riding a bike, running, and general skill confidence. Therefore, children asked to walk, jog or sprint in PE may need a lot of support, especially in relation to their involvement with other children in the class. Consequently, the need for internal maps of the environment is critical, especially as vision is such a rich resource in PE for spatial awareness, observation of movement of self and others that it can leave such children with significant difficulties. These pupils may need the support of a teaching assistant to help them build their confidence.

Children who are **deaf** also require modification of their PE lessons and generally present with movement difficulties. They have specific needs, especially as they are cut off from the environment of your own and fellow pupils' world of sound. This will necessitate specific interventions on the part of the teacher and it will also have an impact on their learning of language. Some deaf children will have conductive hearing loss, which involves the transmission of sound through vibrations to the inner ear, whilst others have sensory neural damage, which hinders perceptual information systems. Deafness tends to be identified on a number of dimensions, such as intensity and quality of sound, and it is vital that prior to any adaptation of PE activities you are clear about what the specific needs of each child are.

There is some evidence to show that children who have inner ear problems have some difficulties in balance, but this generally tends to not be a major issue and rather it is the challenges in relation to presentation and communication of tasks that need most consideration. The onus is therefore on you as the teacher to either be competent in sign language or have support in activities that require significant communication. Feedback, explanation, directions, and demonstrations are also important and will need careful consideration in order to ensure successful PE experiences.

Children with social, emotional and behavioural difficulties

Children who fall into this group range from those who are withdrawn and reclusive through to those who are overly active, lack concentration, appear intentionally aggressive, destructive, and even violent. The Elton Report (DES 1989) suggested that the main types of emotional and behavioural problems in school are those that are described as low intensity–high frequency. That is, the behaviour is not particularly serious but it happens regularly and impacts on the child concerned, other pupils, and the teacher. It is also important to note that many children with social, emotional, and behavioural difficulties (SEBD) also experience communication difficulties (see Parow 2009), which can compound challenges to planning and delivering a PE curriculum that meets the needs and utilises the capabilities of these children.

It is important not to see behavioural problems in isolation from the context within which they take place, and consequently the teacher and the school can determine the nature and degree of incidence. In any PE lesson the teacher has control of the context within which learning takes place and factors such as rules, rewards, punishments and how they are applied are critical. Consequently, blame should not be seen as an issue for extensive debate but rather the focus should be what needs to be organised in order to ensure that the nature of intervention and support for the individual children concerned is consistent and sufficiently decisive that both pupil and teacher know what the ground rules are.

Children with other needs

In discussing the range of needs found amongst children with SEND there will always be children who do not neatly fit into any category, and nor should they.

There are children whose characteristics are idiosyncratic and yet they overlap with difficulties already noted earlier in this chapter. For example, children with **attention deficit disorder (with or without hyperactivity) (ADHD)** have great difficulty in attending to relevant information, are easily distracted, and have short attention spans, which can be accompanied by excessive motor activity and/or hyperactivity. Intervention for these children ranges from medication through to diet, behaviour modification, and educational programmes.

For those children who struggle with attention spans, PE can offer many activities that require short periods of concentration, such as performing gymnastic and dance routines. This, along with interventions elsewhere in the child's schooling, can go a significant way to ensuring learning occurs for these children. In relation to behavioural difficulties, encouraging children to take leadership roles and to conform to rules and regulations can help support them with understanding their particular difficulties. Furthermore, research shows that the most important aspect of supporting such children is a consistent approach to the child's management and support, both within and outside of school. Professionals such as educational psychologists will often play a part in establishing behavioural support systems.

Autism and **Asperger's syndrome** are two further conditions that are more commonly noted by teachers and support assistants in PE (see Maher 2017). Autism involves a number of needs, including language and communication skills, social and personal skills, and stereotypical rhythmic activities. These contribute to posing many challenges for teachers in whatever aspect of schooling they are involved. Asperger's syndrome is a condition that is closely related to autism but these children tend to have improved cognitive and language skills; however, there is evidence that they tend to be clumsy with their motor skills.

Conclusion

In reflecting upon all the characteristics and ranges of SEND described within this chapter, it is hoped that the key message that comes over is that children are individual, unique human beings. As a result, whilst the information offered in this chapter will help you with some initial ideas and thoughts it in no way intends to replace the need for consultation, negotiation and flexibility with the child and all those who support them. PE can be a highly positive experience for all children, whatever their range of needs and characteristics. The key for you is to have an open mind and seize the opportunity to be challenged to think creatively to support the children you work with.

Chapter 4

The physical education National Curriculum and inclusion

Introduction

The subject of PE has been at the centre of many changes since its inception during the early 1990s, especially in relation to its recognition, prominence, and delivery within the NC. In the primary sector, the introduction of the numeracy and literacy hours in the late 1990s brought about a significant squeeze on the time available for other subject areas. In addition, the implementation of the Key Stage Three strategy and its focus on English, Maths, and Science from September 2002, brought with it similar issues and pressures for PE within the secondary sector.

In noting this, however, the NC (2000) did advocate an entitlement of two hours of physical activity within the school week for all children. Furthermore, the Government's PESSCL strategy (DfES/DCMS 2002) supported the development of physical activity by dedicating £459 million from central government funding. In addition, by 2010 the PE, School Sport and Club Links (PESSCL) strategy aimed to offer all children at least four hours of sport every week, comprising at least two hours of high-quality PE and sport at school and the opportunity for at least a further two to three hours beyond the school day (delivered by a range of school, community, and club providers). *Playing to Win: A New Era for Sport* (DCMS 2008) announced a restructuring of sport provision in England and the transition from PESSCL to a new strategy named PESSYP. Here, the Labour Government's new ambition was that all children and young people aged between 5 and 16 years should have the opportunity to participate in five hours of sport per week by 2011, including two hours of high-quality PE and sport at school (DCMS 2008). However, the installation of a Coalition government in 2010 signaled the end of PESSYP. The then Secretary of State for Education, Michael Gove, announced that the Department for Education would cease proving ring-fenced funding in order to give schools the time and freedom to focus on providing competitive sport (Phillpots 2013). Naturally, children with SEND had the same entitlement, and teachers and schools were expected to ensure that their needs were met alongside all other pupils.

This chapter sets out to examine the NC for PE (DfE 2014a) and its relevance to children with SEND. In addition to examining the purpose, aims, attainment targets, and subject content, it will look at the principles of the statutory inclusion statement and the expectations that are placed on schools and teachers alike. The subject of PE will be analysed in relation to its structure, organisation, and delivery, and potential to link to wider sporting opportunities as part of an examination of 'disability sports' activities.

The chapter concludes by highlighting a range of issues and themes that are emerging related to ensuring that PE teachers are sufficiently equipped to include children with SEND within mainstream settings. As with all the other chapters, and what can be seen as a central theme to this book, this chapter highlights the need for teachers to approach tasks with flexibility, high expectations of children with SEND and a willingness to engage in modification and adaptation as a crucial element in ensuring successful outcomes for the individuals concerned.

Defining and interpreting PE

According to DfE (2014a: 103):

> A high-quality physical education curriculum inspires all pupils to succeed and excel in competitive sport and other physically-demanding activities. It should provide opportunities for pupils to become physically confident in a way which supports their health and fitness. Opportunities to compete in sport and other activities build character and help to embed values such as fairness and respect.

From the statement above, it is evident that competitive sport has been repositioned at the center of PE. This is of particular interest given that research suggests that teachers (see Morley et al. 2005) and LSAs (see Maher 2017) have questioned the compatibility of competitive sport ideologies and ideologies of inclusion. Therefore, it is perhaps even more crucial that teachers have the knowledge, skills, and experiences to plan and deliver learning opportunities that are both inclusive and competitive.

Whilst there is still an expectation that teachers provide a broad and balanced curriculum, teachers are not constrained to deliver the six activity areas that were emphasised in previous curriculums. Only dance and outdoor and adventurous activities (OAA) remain at Key Stage 3, and OAA on its own at Key Stage 4. This gives teachers and schools greater influence over the type of activities used to facilitate learning, but teachers should be mindful of the importance of experiencing a broad, varied and balanced curriculum so that pupils can make informed choices about the type of activities they want to participate in outside of school and once their compulsory education ends.

Provision, as part of the NC 2014, should be made available to all children, including those with SEND. As a result, teachers will often need to think in different ways about what and how they are going to teach, whilst making best use of their differentiation, teaching and learning strategies. Sugden and Talbot (1998) support this view, and suggest that teaching children with SEND is merely an extension of teachers' mixed ability teaching. Thus, flexibility of teaching and learning strategy is central to successful inclusive PE. This view is similar to that of Dyson and Millward (2000), Ainscow et al. (1999), and Skrtic (1995), which places the emphasis for change on teachers, and stresses the need for them to be pro-active and adapt the curriculum to meet the individual needs of children with SEND.

At Key Stage 3, The NC 2014 states that pupils should be taught to:

- use a range of tactics and strategies to overcome opponents in direct competition through team and individual games;
- develop their technique and improve their performance in other competitive sports;
- perform dances using advanced dance techniques within a range of dance styles and forms;
- take part in outdoor and adventurous activities that present intellectual and physical challenges and be encouraged to work in a team, building on trust and developing skills to solve problems, either individually or as a group;
- analyse their performances compared to previous ones and demonstrate improvement to achieve their personal best;
- take part in competitive sports and activities outside school through community links or sports clubs.

This subject content, delivered through a choice of activity areas, and with acknowledgement of the principles of the Statutory Inclusion Statement (i.e. setting suitable challenges and responding to pupils' needs and overcoming potential barriers for individuals and groups of pupils) establish the context for the implementation of the PE curriculum in primary, secondary and special schools.

Task 4.1　The subject content for PE

Reflect upon the subject content of the PE NC 2014 and consider what issues you may need to address in order to effectively include children with SEND.

PE NC content area	Issues that need to be considered for children with SEND
Use a range of tactics and strategies to overcome opponents in direct competition through team and individual games	
Develop their technique and improve their performance in other competitive sports	
Perform dances using advanced dance techniques within a range of dance styles and forms	
Take part in outdoor and adventurous activities that present intellectual and physical challenges and be encouraged to work in a team, building on trust and developing skills to solve problems, either individually or as a group	
Analyse their performances compared to previous ones and demonstrate improvement to achieve their personal best	
Take part in competitive sports and activities outside school through community links or sports clubs	

The National Curriculum for PE and children with SEND

The revised NC for PE (2014) (DfE 2014a) suggests teachers should set challenging but achievable assessments, with flexible judgements and an understanding of contexts in order to facilitate access to the curriculum for pupils with SEND. It states, 'lessons should be planned to ensure that there are no barriers to every pupil achieving' (DfE 2014a: 8) and be responsive to a diverse range of pupil needs in order to facilitate inclusive education. In meeting these requirements, teachers will need to actively review their pedagogical practices in order to ensure they meet the statutory requirements to facilitate entitlement and accessibility to inclusive activities for all pupils, including those with SEND.

In order to satisfactorily address the needs of pupils with SEND, Farrell suggests teachers must be willing to move beyond an acknowledgment of inclusion policies and be prepared 'to reconsider their structure, teaching approaches, pupil grouping and use of support' (Farrell 1998: 81). This position supports work noted by Ainscow (1999) who advocates a notion of 'moving schools' that are constantly evolving and changing to be responsive to the needs of the pupils it serves.

The four key principles related to equality, identified in the 1992 NC for PE (DES 1992b), still hold true today as guiding principles when including pupils with SEND within mainstream PE (Vickerman and Hayes 2013). These are **entitlement, accessibility, integration and integrity**, and have acted as the cornerstones upon which the NC for PE (2014) has been revised. In relation to **entitlement**, the premise is to acknowledge the fundamental right of pupils with SEND to access the PE curriculum. This is of particular relevance with the emergence of the SEN and Disability Rights Act (DfES 2001c), which gives pupils a fundamental right to inclusive activity, and the revised *Code of Practice* (DfE/DoH 2015). The *Code of Practice* now focuses on the action of schools and teachers to implement and deliver inclusive PE through greater consultation with parents and pupils, and thinking in different ways about teaching provision.

Teachers are expected therefore to take action within their individual school contexts, and modify and adapt practices in order to facilitate full entitlement to the curriculum for pupils with SEND. This shift in legislation recognises the philosophy of positive attitudes and open minds (Vickerman 2002), and the commitment to a process that offers inclusive education, in which teachers overcome potential barriers through consultation and the adoption of diverse learning, teaching and assessment strategies. This position is to some extent reflected in the Teachers' Standards (DfE 2013a) with the expectation that trainee teachers will demonstrate evidence of differentiated teaching, response to pupils' diverse learning needs, and the promotion of positive values.

In terms of **accessibility,** it is the responsibility of teachers to make PE lessons accessible and relevant to the child with SEND. This supports the social model of disability (Reiser and Mason 1990) in which teachers adjust their teaching in order to accommodate the needs of individual pupils rather than the child's disability (medical model) being seen as the barrier to participation and learning. In examining the need to make PE lessons relevant and accessible, it is important to acknowledge the earlier view of Sugden and Talbot (1998), who suggest that teaching pupils with SEND is part of an extension of mixed ability teaching. Teachers should therefore possess many of the skills necessary to facilitate inclusive PE, and consequently may only occasionally require specialist advice and guidance.

Thus, the fundamental factor in a successful inclusive activity for pupils with SEND is a positive attitude (Haegele et al. 2016), suitable differentiation and a readiness to modify existing practice within PE lessons (Maher 2016). Whilst there may be a few difficulties for teachers to embrace more inclusive approaches, the PE profession is well placed to embrace inclusive practice, and to a large extent the process has begun with the increased focus on aspects of inclusion within PE, education and society in general.

However, the critical success factors in the drive to more inclusive PE will be the training and support given to trainee teachers, newly qualified teachers and schools within process models which reflect implementation of 'policy through to practice' (Depauw and Doll-Tepper 2000). As a result, ITT providers, schools and statutory agencies need to ensure that future teachers are adequately prepared to deliver this inclusive agenda. Consequently, greater levels of multi-agency and collaborative working practices are required in the years ahead.

The third principle of **integration** recognises the benefits of children with and without SEND being educated together and the positive outcomes, which can be achieved for all pupils through such approaches. Whilst concepts of integration have moved on since 1992 (now embracing concepts of inclusion), these can be seen as fundamental stepping-stones towards inclusive practice (Slininger et al. 2000), ultimately recognising difference but treating pupils appropriately and according to their learning needs and capabilities. This also begins to address the UK Government's citizenship agenda in which pupils are to be educated to have mutual understanding and respect for individual diversity as part of their involvement and participation within a socially inclusive society. PE is an ideal vehicle for this to occur, with many activities involving teamwork and co-operation.

PE teachers need to underpin their learning and teaching practice with **integrity**, and a recognition that they value and believe in the adaptations and changes that are made to the activities they teach. As part of this personal commitment, they should ensure that inclusive PE for pupils with SEND is of equal worth, challenging, and in no way patronising or demeaning to the individual child concerned. PE teachers should therefore adopt approaches that set appropriate and challenging tasks (NC 2014 Inclusion Statement (DfE 2014a)) to pupils who have additional learning needs whilst avoiding the 'cotton wool' approach, which often assumes that these pupils cannot cope with some of the demands that a challenging curriculum may offer (Vickerman and Hayes 2013). Consequently, this may involve schools and teachers re-examining their present teaching philosophies, attitudes, values, and cultures with the intention of establishing flexible yet challenging educational experiences for children with SEND (Booth et al. 2000).

Task 4.2   Principles of equality of opportunity

Reflect on the four principles of entitlement, accessibility, integration and integrity and develop your understanding of each of these, then look at what you will need to do to ensure children with SEND gain positive experiences in their PE lessons.

Adapted PE and sport

In conjunction with definitions, interpretations, and contexts related to the PE curriculum in the UK, extensive work has been undertaken in the development of 'adapted PE', 'adapted sport', and 'disability sport' both in the UK and in the USA.

Principles of equality of opportunity in PE	Your interpretation of the principle	Action you need to take to ensure children gain positive outcomes
Entitlement		
Accessibility		
Integration		
Integrity		

These strategies support and extend provision within the formal school curriculum, and have to a certain extent shaped the delivery of present day PE and school sport for children with SEND. Winnick and Porretta (2017) suggest that adapted PE is a sub-discipline of PE that allows for safe, personally satisfying and successful participation to meet the unique needs of students.

Adapted PE is designed to meet the long-term (i.e. over 30 days) unique needs of children with disabilities, and establish common frameworks for their inclusion within PE programmes (Roth et al. 2017; Winnick and Porretta 2017). As Winnick and Porretta (2017: 4) say, 'Adapted physical education is an individualised program of physical and motor fitness; fundamental motor skills and patterns; and skills . . . designed to meet the unique needs of individuals'.

In contrast:

> Adapted sport refers to sport modified or created to meet the unique needs of individuals. Based on this definition, for example, basketball is a general sport and wheelchair basketball is an adapted sport . . . Individuals with disabilities may participate in general sport or adapted sport conducted in unified, segregated, individualized and parallel settings.
>
> (Winnick and Porretta 2017: 6)

The use of the term 'adapted sport' is preferred to 'disability sport' as it stimulates and encourages participation and excellence in a variety of settings, rather than categorising activity that specifically caters for disabled people alone (Roth et al. 2017; Depauw and Gavron 2005; Winnick and Porretta 2017). This supports a shift towards inclusive activity in which children with SEND participate within the same inclusive environment as their age-peers. To some extent, this shift is also being seen within national and international disability sport – for example, adults in the London 2012 and Rio 2016 Olympics competed at the same venue and at the same time.

Roth et al. (2017) argue within the contexts of adapted PE and sport that it is crucial for teachers to assume responsibility for all children and adults that they work with, regardless of individual needs. Winnick and Porretta support this view in suggesting:

A good teacher and/or coach of children recognises the development of positive self-esteem as important and displays an attitude of acceptance, empathy, friendship and warmth, while ensuring a secure and controlled environment. The good teacher or coach of adapted physical education and sport selects and uses teaching approaches and styles beneficial to students, provides individualised and personalised instruction and opportunities, and creates a positive environment where students can succeed.

(Winnick and Porretta 2017: 8)

This supports the current thinking on the practice, structure and delivery of inclusion within the UK in which flexibility, adaptation and openness to change are seen as critical success factors (Dyson and Millward 2000; Ainscow 1999; Skrtic 1991, 1995).

Developing practice in inclusive PE and sport

Whilst the most significant progress in adapted activity has recently focused on educational services for children and adults with disabilities, the use of physical activity as part of exercise and therapy for treatment is not a new concept, and dates back to as early as 3000 BC in China. The Romans and Greeks also recognised the benefits of therapy and the value of exercise as a means of assisting with mobility and general health and well-being (Winnick and Porretta 2017; Roth et al. 2017). Developments in physical activity and remedial therapy date back many years and have contributed to arriving at more contemporary approaches to inclusive PE and sport for children with SEND. Sherrill (2004) notes that the 1800s and early part of the 1900s, for example, were initially characterised by medical orientation of therapy, prevention, rehabilitation and cure.

However, there was a shift from the 1930s to the modern day, and now thinking has shifted from the medical to the 'whole person' approach, which runs in tandem with educational developments moving from segregated to inclusive, person-centred strategies. Within the context of 'whole person orientations', Winnick and Porretta (2017) suggest individuals who require physical activity programmes as part of their disability should be assessed according to their particular needs, then programmes should be established that best fit their individual needs. This is in line with modern day concepts of inclusive practice within schools, in which teachers and schools change and adapt their provision to meet the individual needs of children with SEND, rather than the other way around.

In shifting to more inclusive practices, Winnick and Porretta (2017) established a framework of 'alternative instructional placements' within the PE curriculum that were based on strategies moving from conventional medical models of treatment and separate centres, which were described as 'most restrictive', through to 'regular' inclusive placements, which were 'least restrictive' in terms of developing the child with SEND as a whole. 'Least restrictive environments', according to Winnick and Porretta (2017), require teachers to focus upon the curriculum, teaching styles, and organisational strategies. In facilitating an inclusive (least restrictive) curriculum, for example, lessons should be based on developmentally appropriate activities, centred upon 'Craft's (1996) four curricula options', namely:

- **same curriculum** – access to the same activity areas within the curriculum;
- **multi-level curriculum** – pursuing different objectives, but within the same lesson;
- **curriculum overlap** – involving modification of the curriculum;
- **alternative curriculum** – separate or disability specific activities.

Thus, there is an expectation that teachers adopt a range of flexible teaching, learning and organisational approaches to deliver inclusive PE for children with SEND (DfE 2013a). Craft's (1996) 'curricula options' complement recent thinking in the development of the 'inclusion spectrum', which builds upon Winnick and Porretta's notion of flexible teaching and learning strategies and has been extended by the Youth Sport Trust and the EFDS. The inclusion spectrum offers a range of strategies that teachers can move in and out of during their lessons in order to ensure maximum participation and access to physical activity for children with SEND. These strategies are, however, not solely

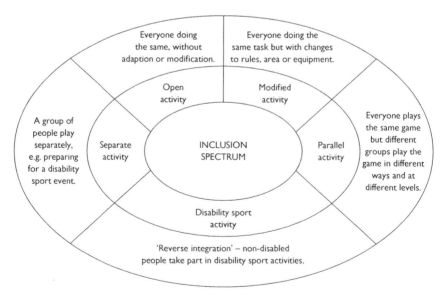

Figure 4.1 The inclusion spectrum.

(Source: Youth Sport Trust)

related to including children with SEND and can be used to create greater flexibility in teaching and learning to include all pupils. The inclusion spectrum suggests five strategies of open, modified, parallel, separate, and disability sport activities that enable teachers to deliver PE in conjunction with the principles of the NC (2014) Inclusion Statement (DfE 2014a) (see Figure 4.1).

Task 4.3   The range of teaching and learning strategies

Reflect upon the range of teaching and learning strategies discussed to date in this chapter and consider which you feel will fit best with the pupils you teach and your personal teaching philosophies and ideologies.

Extending and developing teaching and learning strategies in PE

As part of their general teaching philosophy and practices, teachers should seek to embrace the guiding principles of entitlement, accessibility, integration and integrity. This should be undertaken alongside contemporary notions of inclusion and flexible teaching and learning strategies if teachers are to make a genuine commitment to inclusive PE for pupils with SEND. Additionally, as part of the revised NC for PE (2014) (DfE 2014a), teachers need to spend time interpreting the Inclusion Statement, whilst recognising the need to set suitable learning challenges, respond to pupils' diverse needs, and overcome potential barriers to learning and assessment for individuals and groups of pupils. The strategies and models offered in the 'four curricula options' (Craft 1996), 'inclusion spectrum', and 'continuum of alternative instructional placements in physical education' (Winnick and Porretta, 2017) are valuable starting points for teachers to consider their approach to inclusive PE.

In relation to **'setting suitable learning challenges'**, the NC for PE (2014) (DfE 2014a: 9) states that:

> Teachers should set high expectations for every pupil. They should plan stretching work for pupils whose attainment is significantly above the expected standard. They have an even greater obligation to plan lessons for pupils who have low levels of prior attainment or come from disadvantaged backgrounds. Teachers should use appropriate assessment to set targets which are deliberately ambitious.

This can be achieved by teaching knowledge, skills, and understanding of PE from earlier key stages, if appropriate, with the aim of ensuring those pupils with SEND progress and achieve. It could be argued, therefore, that inclusion for pupils with SEND is about focusing upon earlier developmental expectations, or adopting a more flexible teaching approach to accommodate individuals' needs in terms of learning, teaching and assessment. Sugden and Talbot (1998), for example, support this view through the principles of 'moving to learn' and 'learning to move'. They argue: 'Physical education has a distinctive role to play, because it is not simply about education of the physical but involves cognitive, social, language and moral development and responsibilities' (Sugden and Talbot 1998: 22). Thus, to facilitate inclusion, a shift away from the traditional (learning to move) outcome of PE in which skills are taught and learned, to a wider experience of PE (moving to learn) which focuses on the physical, cognitive, affective, and social domains of learning may be one such approach in enabling access to inclusive PE.

PE teachers need to consider their learning outcomes carefully in order to ensure all pupils with SEND have the opportunity to demonstrate a wide variety of movement learning experiences, and this links with the principle of **'responding to pupils' learning needs'**. Consequently, the NC for PE (2014) suggests that teachers should plan and deliver lessons in ways that ensure that there are no barriers to pupil achievement, especially those with SEND (DfE 2014a).

This section suggests lessons should be planned to ensure full and effective access, and that teachers need to be aware of equal opportunity legislation. This begins to answer some of Dyson's (1999) concerns that the curriculum needs to focus on how outcomes can be differentiated and measured for each child, rather than focusing upon philosophical definitions of equality. A key feature is that this will need to be based upon the social model of disability and a commitment to change the activity to fit the child rather than the other way around (Vickerman 2010).

In terms of **'overcoming potential barriers to learning and assessment for individuals and groups of pupils'** the NC for PE (2014) suggests a minority of pupils will have particular learning and assessment requirements that go beyond the provisions described earlier (sections one and two) so may need access to specialist equipment and different approaches (DfE 2014a). The curriculum suggests that in creating access, greater differentiation on the part of teachers and the use of external agencies or specialist equipment will begin to enable inclusion to occur. This statement is fundamental in ensuring that teachers recognise their full responsibility for creating accessible lessons that cater for all pupils' needs, whilst recognising the need to work through a multi-agency approach to deliver inclusive activities (Depauw and Doll-Tepper 2000). This means teachers will need to have different expectations of some pupils with SEND, and/or will need to modify assessment in ways that offer children the opportunity to demonstrate development of their knowledge and understanding.

The strategies outlined so far aim to move in the direction of 'least restrictive' activities within a context of support within 'regular', inclusive environments.

This changing teaching philosophy reflects many of the legislative changes that have occurred over recent years to support this practice (Equality Act 2010; Children and Families Act 2014; Code of Practice 2015; NC 2014). Within this backdrop the modern day approach to physical activity for adults with disabilities and children with SEND is to work towards an integration continuum for sport participation that supports regular (inclusive), rather than segregated (restrictive), provision (Winnick 1987). The model indicated in the earlier work of Winnick (1987) succinctly emphasises the context within which inclusive education for children with SEND should be established in the future.

In reviewing the diverse range of teaching and learning models designed for the inclusion of children with SEND in PE, it could be argued that they can be grouped into three categories (Block and Volger 1994; Giangreco et al. 1993). These are based around:

- **curriculum adaptation** – changing what is taught;
- **instructional modifications** – changing how we teach;
- **human or people resources** – looking at changing who teaches or supports adapted aspects of PE.

Statutory agencies, teacher training providers, schools, trainee teachers, and practitioners should structure their future training and development around these three factors in order to progress inclusion for children with SEND.

Many of the early studies undertaken into good practice identify critical success factors related to teaching and learning, yet are patchier in gauging the views and opinions of children with SEND related to their experiences of inclusive PE (Dyson and Millward 2000; Ainscow 1999; Skrtic 1991, 1995; Volger and Romance 2000; Slininger et al. 2000). However, Goodwin and Watkinson (2000) identified a distinction between what they refer to as 'good days and bad days' for children with SEND in inclusive PE. The study found children with SEND who were involved in positive, inclusive PE experiences described the 'good days' as being engaged in learning contexts with modified practices to accommodate their needs, feelings of progression in skill development, sense of belonging, and the support of teachers who were prepared to adopt flexible approaches to their involvement. These experiences support many of the issues noted earlier based upon curriculum adaptation, instructional modifications and human resources. In contrast, 'bad days' involved restricted participation (Winnick 2000) in which, due to a lack of flexibility of approach, children with SEND felt isolated, demotivated, lacking in self-esteem and engaged in learning environments where teachers had not planned effectively for their involvement.

In support of these findings, Place and Hodge (2001) looked at the behaviour of children with and without disabilities when engaged in inclusive PE related to levels of social interaction between the two groups of children. They found inclusive PE can lead to increased social interaction, but only if there is full recognition and due regard for inclusive PE as a process, which is practised within a context of:

- **appropriate curricula adaptations** – recognising and valuing diversity, and planning effectively for its implementation;
- **instructional modifications** – based upon sound pedagogical practices that enhance rather than restrict inclusive activity;
- **sound human resources** – incorporating PE teachers who are well equipped to deliver inclusive PE;
- **informed decision-making** – based on consultation, reflection, and a readiness to modify and adapt strategies to facilitate inclusive activity.

Slininger et al. (2000) support this view in their advocation of 'contact theory' in which they argue that, in order to eliminate prejudice and discrimination, and establish environments that are conducive to learning, teachers must plan effectively for inclusive lessons. They found that if teachers did not plan inclusive lessons, many shared opportunities for learning and development were missed and the overall success of inclusive learning was limited. This research demonstrates the need for teachers to spend time planning effectively for inclusion within a context of readiness to change, and modify existing teaching and learning strategies. Chapter 9 will draw on more contemporary research to explore the PE experiences of pupils with SEND from their own perspective.

Practical examples of inclusive PE for children with SEND

When planning inclusive PE for pupils with SEND it is important to start from the premise of full inclusion, and, where this may not be possible, to consider adaptation or modification of learning and teaching activities (Winnick and Porretta 2017). A central success factor for teachers is to consult, where appropriate, with the child with SEND and relevant professionals as part of a multidisciplinary approach. This enables the pupil and teachers to consider, at the planning stage, any differentiation that may be required (Goodwin and Watkinson 2000). This supports principles of equality and the social model approach, which acknowledges individual diversity whilst also responding to the needs of pupils with SEND by modifying or adapting activities as appropriate.

An example of this could be in games activities such as hockey, where pupils may initially require lighter, larger or different coloured balls in order to access the activity. Adaptations to rules may need to be considered, such as allowing a player with movement restrictions five seconds to receive and play the ball. If utilising such a strategy, it is vital that all members of the group understand the need for such an adaptation (Sherrill 2004) in order that they can play to this rule during a game. In dance, activities can be adapted through consultation with pupils with and without SEND as part of the requirements of the curriculum to work co-operatively. A pupil who requires a wheelchair for mobility, for example, can use the chair as an extension of their body to move around a particular area. If group tasks are to be performed, then the group can work together on themes for inclusion in which the movement patterns of the pupils with SEND can be incorporated into the overall group piece being performed (Vickerman and Hayes 2013).

Another example of inclusive participation in athletic activities with pupils with physical disabilities may involve one push of their wheelchair, rather than a jump into the sandpit, or reducing distances to run or travel. If there are pupils with visual impairments teachers can organise activities such as a 100-metre race in which a guide stands at the finish line and shouts out the lane number they are in, or a guide runs alongside them for support. Many of the suggestions indicated above support the points noted earlier of needing to be open to change whilst recognising that this work is as an integral component of a PE teacher's general mixed ability teaching (Sugden and Talbot 1998). Consequently, the attitude of mind and motivation to change existing teaching and learning practices is central to successful inclusive activity (Dyson and Millward 2000).

Concluding thoughts and a rationale for inclusive PE

The NC for PE (2014) clearly supports the notion of inclusion through a set of statements that are based upon ensuring that teachers set suitable learning challenges; respond to pupils' diverse learning needs; and overcome potential barriers to learning and assessment in order to accommodate all children's needs. However, in setting out to achieve such an inclusive approach, Dyson (1999) noted some concern that the concept of disability may become 'at the heart of a new and privileged society' (Dyson 1999: 2).

According to Dyson, 'social inclusion' is limited as it only pursues measures to remove difference that focus upon predicted equality, and are not necessarily outcome based. Therefore, implementation of policies by government agencies and schools may appear to be socially and morally right, but the danger is that measurement will be through expectations for statements written into policies. However, success should be judged in terms of its impact and effects upon a child's quality of education and achievement. (See Depauw and Doll-Tepper (2000), Dyson (2001), and Farrell (2000, 2001) for further issues related to policy implementation and practice.) Thus, greater focus in the future must be turned to the development of facilitating inclusive practice through pedagogical practices, rather than simply making policy statements of intent.

On examining the inclusion statement in relation to PE, these fundamental requirements, in conjunction with recent legislative changes, will require PE teachers to ensure they are fulfilling all their statutory and professional practice responsibilities. As a consequence, teachers need to ensure they facilitate and empower children with SEND to have full entitlement and accessibility to the curriculum.

Dyson (1999) supports such a move as part of the process model that moves beyond recognition of principles and philosophical standpoints and into the

Key aspects to consider in moving from philosophy to action	Review your understanding of the terms	Action required as part of your teaching and learning strategies
What are key principles?		
What are philosophical standpoints?		
What is action-based practice?		
What is a curriculum that relates to outcomes differentiated for each child?		
What are strategies for consultation?		

practice of action based upon how the curriculum relates to outcomes that can be differentiated and measured for each child. A key feature of this occurring will need to be based upon a strong emphasis of consultation between teachers, pupils with SEND, parents and professionals (Vickerman 2010). This will need to be undertaken within the context of models of best practice in teaching and learning in inclusive education noted earlier (Dyson 2001; Winnick and Porretta 2017).

Task 4.4   Process models of inclusive practice

Reflect upon Dyson's (1999) view of inclusion for children with SEND in PE needing to be part of a process model that moves from philosophy to action-based practice. Use the table below to review your understanding of the process model and what strategies you may employ in PE to ensure successful experiences for children with SEND.

Given the increasing onus placed on teachers to be(come) inclusive educators, a greater focus on the consideration of models of best practice in teaching and learning pedagogy will need to be considered and shared by all teachers within the profession. However, you as an individual can make a difference to children with SEND and you should remember to both stimulate discussion with colleagues whilst ensuring your practice meets the needs of the children concerned.

Chapter 5

Planning for and assessing children with special educational needs and disabilities

Introduction

This chapter sets out to review the strategies that are necessary for planning for and assessing children with SEND in PE. In any PE lesson the importance of setting suitable learning challenges through clear expectations, knowledge of individual children, flexibility, and a commitment to modification and adaptive practices is essential. As a result, if we plan our teaching and objectives around these central principles we should employ the same strategies in relation to assessing children with SEND. This chapter will help you to review your understanding of what, why and how we assess children in PE, whilst assisting you to consider diverse strategies to ensure individuals have the best chance to demonstrate competence in PE.

Assessment should be considered as a process, which gives both the child with SEND and the teacher an insight into learning that is associated with a permanent change in the behaviour of the learner. In order to ascertain whether learning in PE has taken place, it must be assessed to see if the learning outcomes have been achieved. It is through this process that teachers provide a constructive foundation for future planning and target setting of pupils with SEND. Furthermore, assessment provides a valuable activity for teachers in judging their own teaching, learning and planning, and highlighting effective and ineffective aspects of this process. Thus, assessment can act as a dual strategy both to assist the pupil with SEND and to enable the teacher to quantify their own learning and development.

A central tenet of this dual assessment process is the need for teachers to be aware of the second and third aspects of the PE NC Statutory Inclusion Statement. These require teachers to respond to pupils' diverse needs (thus requiring flexibility in assessment design) and to overcome potential barriers to learning and assessment for individuals and groups of pupils. As a result, teachers deliver this by getting to know the individual needs of children and ensuring that assessment strategies are established to help children with SEND demonstrate knowledge and understanding of PE through flexible approaches rather than being highly prescriptive about the specific method to be utilised.

When should assessment take place for children with SEND?

Assessment is critical to the learning of new skills and understanding how this information can be utilised to progress learning for children with SEND. It is important, therefore, to ensure that every child, regardless of their ability and range of SEND, is working to their full potential. This will require teachers to have a good knowledge of the individual needs of children and a commitment to be adaptable and have high expectations of what children with SEND can achieve. As movement is a central component of PE and is very often assessed, many of the examples in this chapter will be drawn from this setting in order to exemplify your understanding of the process.

According to Newton and Bowler (2010), assessment includes activities performed by teachers and others to gauge the effectiveness of teaching and learning. Consequently, assessment in PE takes place for many reasons, for example in selecting or grouping pupils, as an indicator of how well a task or concept is understood, to motivate pupils, monitor progress, or more generally to give feedback to teacher, pupil and parents. However, an important issue to consider as part of any assessment strategy is to ask the question, for what purposes do we need to collect, analyse, store and retrieve data? Thus it is important that it helps to determine how information will be meaningful to the pupil, teacher and parent rather than just fulfilling the school assessment policy. This view is supported by Frapwell et al. (2002: 24), who state, 'To view assessment as divorced from the planning, teaching and learning process results in the implementation of a meaningless bolt on model, a bureaucratic monster or a task to satisfy senior management requirements'.

If assessment is to play an important role in the teaching and learning process it should not be seen as purely a 'bolt on' process; in contrast, it needs to be seen as an activity that has the potential to occur all the time in the PE lesson. This is known as 'formative assessment', which means it is ongoing throughout their lesson and helps both you as the teacher and the child gain insight into how they are doing at any particular point in the lesson. Formative feedback is a vital aspect of any assessment process as it offers ongoing, current, situational and contextual feedback at a time when the child understands and appreciates it. For children with SEND, formative feedback is especially important because teachers need to identify a pupil's movement concepts and motor skills, what the body does in specific contexts, where the body moves, how the body moves and with whom or with what the body moves. It is vital that these basic movement patterns are established for children with poor motor skills in particular, in order to move onto more specialist skills. Thus, a child might have good control when using small movements, but large motor movements, such as catching or kicking a ball, may prove more difficult. The assessment strategy needs to identify these children and their specific needs in order to minimise frustration and so that negativity and fear of failure do not set in on the part of the individual concerned.

Task 5.1   Why and how we assess

Use the table below to review your thoughts on why we assess and how we use the data to help our understanding of the needs of children with SEND in PE.

What is it that we should be assessing in PE?

Developing and supporting children's movement patterns is a critical part of PE and wider life and social skills, which include activities such as walking, jogging, sprinting, throwing and catching a ball, and jumping. These movement patterns can be described through the analysis and description of definitive arrangements of muscle actions, which are required to fulfil the desired outcomes in any lesson. However, assessment is not just about observing movement patterns and motor skills, rather it can be described as an integrated process that builds up a picture of the whole child.

A significant amount of work on movement has been influenced by Laban's framework (see Laban 1942) and this considers movement to be not only of prime importance in the shaping of attitudes and relationships but also a vital force in education. Bailey (1999) supports this view by suggesting that there is little doubting the central importance of movement and physical activity in the lives of children and young people. In his research he found physical play was the first appearing and most frequently occurring expression in infants and physical competence as a second and major factor that influences social acceptance in children of all ages and both sexes. Thus, there is a need to build a picture of the strengths and weaknesses of children with SEND; not just in relation to motor skills but how this affects the child emotionally and whether

Aspects of assessment	Your understanding of the issues
Why do we assess?	
For what purposes do we need to collect information?	
What do you understand by responding to pupils' diverse needs in assessment?	
How can you overcome potential barriers to learning and assessment for individuals and groups of pupils?	
How and why do we analyse information on children with SEND?	
How and why do we store assessment data?	
For what purposes should we retrieve and report assessment data?	

self-concept, self-esteem and motivation levels are impacted upon as well. Consequently, when teachers work with children with SEND they should be asking questions such as:

- Is a lack of motor skills affecting other areas of learning?
- Does a lack of motor skills affect the child's interaction with others?
- Are children with SEND generally unhappy with their general physical competence?
- Is there other behaviour occurring as a result of the child's difficulty with movement?
- If movement is seen to be enjoyable and meaningful, how does this impact on children's everyday life skills and experiences and are they more likely to achieve success in PE?

In reviewing the questions above with an open mind and commitment to flexible teaching, learning and assessment strategies you will be able to plan for effective inclusion whilst identifying any potential barriers to participation, and then be in a position to take action as required. With regard to assessing children with SEND at the end of PE lessons this supports pupils' learning, motivates pupils through feedback and progress to date and provides a context for the next lesson. This type of formative assessment will help the teacher identify poor motor ability, which can have a serious effect on behaviour and motivation in all areas of the curriculum. If a child with SEND (as with their age-peers) continually experiences failure, frustration will set in, which in turn will lead to individuals becoming demotivated, and they will begin to get into a negative spiral about experiences and participation in PE.

Teachers should also assess at the end of a series of lessons as this helps with the monitoring of pupils' progress and achievement and provides feedback to individuals to help them consolidate their skills over a period of time. This can also be an opportunity for the teacher to give positive feedback to the child about areas of permanent addition to the learning skills and abilities of the individual concerned. Finally, assessment at the end of a year helps in the reviewing of pupils' strengths and identifies areas for development, focuses on activity and personal development, and forms the basis for a report to the pupils and parents about the progress they have made in all aspects of the year's work.

In the NC for PE (2014) attainment targets are used in the assessment of pupils, and they set out what pupils are expected to know, apply and understand in relation to key stage programmes of study. Given that the more prescriptive level descriptors have been removed, it is critical that you approach assessment judgements flexibly and use the attainment targets as a guide for interpretation in relation to individual children with SEND.

At Key Stage 1, pupils should develop fundamental movement skills, become increasingly competent and confident and access a broad range of opportunities to extend their agility, balance and coordination, individually and with others. They should be able to engage in competitive (both against self and against others) and co-operative physical activities, in a range of increasingly challenging situations.

At Key Stage 2, pupils should continue to apply and develop a broader range of skills, learning how to use them in different ways and to link them to make actions and sequences of movement. They should enjoy communicating, collaborating and competing with each other. They should develop an understanding of how to improve in different physical activities and sports and learn how to evaluate and recognise their own success.

In order to use attainment targets, teachers need to adopt flexible assessment strategies to be able to ensure they meet the needs of specific pupils. An example of this could be shown by linking the statements in with the Movement Assessment Battery for Children-2 (MABC-2) (see Henderson et al. 2007). This offers a far more rounded picture of the level the child was working at. The levels include the children describing and commentating on their own work and that of others, which gives the child more 'ownership' of the task. This may also identify the child who actually understands the movement but is not controlled when carrying out the task. At Key Stage 1, pupils should develop fundamental movement skills, which can include using simple games to copy, repeat and explore simple actions such jumping, hopping and skipping activities. These activities will involve various degrees of balance and transfer of weight. The described types of movement underpin much more complex tasks, so by including them in a fun way and showing that the tasks have a purpose they are much more likely to be successful.

If throwing tasks are being practised, using targets of different sizes and different distances is far more enjoyable than throwing at a wall or simply just throwing and catching (sending and receiving). Varying the tasks whilst concentrating on the same skill will stop the child becoming bored and help the teacher to form an overall picture of the level the children are working at and the child's individual needs. Getting the children to describe how their bodies feel during exercise is also helping them to understand what happens to their bodies during physical activity. These actions fit into the visual, audio and kinaesthetic model of learning, and should encourage children to observe themselves and others, listen to feedback, give feedback on their observations, and describe how their bodies feel during the tasks. This enables them to focus and concentrate more on each individual action and is a critical element in encouraging children with SEND to develop confidently and securely in PE.

How can we assess movement?

There are many ways of assessing movement. The NC Key Stage attainment targets should be used alongside MABC-2 with reference to the *Special Educational Needs Code of Practice* (DfE/DoH 2015). AfPE's 'Expert Group' have also developed guidance on assessment which will be of use

(AfPE 2014). The more information that can be gathered, the easier it is to set specific targets that can form the basis of an individual education plan (IEP), which identifies a child's immediate learning needs by assessing a pupil's progress against these targets. This again needs to be a continuous process to ensure progression and indicate what future action might need to be taken. In this respect, it is important to note that Maher (2013) has questioned the relevance of IEPs to PE and PE teachers given that much of the information provided in these plans is not PE-specific. Therefore, PE teachers may need to interpret information that often relates to classroom-based learning environments and translate and apply it to PE. In relation to the *Special Educational Needs Code of Practice*, teachers need to be aware of the nature and level of support required by pupils when making judgements.

SEN support in schools

In most instances, high-quality teaching, which is differentiated based on pupils' needs and capabilities, will support pupils with SEND. However, it is important that teachers and schools take action to remove potential barriers to learning before/when they arise by providing SEN support. According to the *Code of Practice*,

> SEN support should take the form of a four-part cycle [**assess, plan, do and review**] through which earlier decisions and actions are revisited, refined and revised with a growing understanding of the pupil's needs and of what supports the pupil in making good progress and securing good outcomes.
>
> (DfE/DoH 2015: 100)

Each stage of this cycle is explained below:

Assess: When a member of staff identifies a pupil with SEND, the subject teachers in consultation with the special educational needs co-ordinator (SENCO) should conduct an assessment to clearly identify the needs of the pupil. This assessment should draw on the pupil's previous progress and attainment, measured against their age-peers in the school and national data. Information should also be gather from the parents and pupil themselves to gain a more rounded perspective. In some instances, health and social services may be involved with the child. In this instance, they should help inform the assessment.

Plan: When the school decides that formal support is warranted, parents must be informed. The SENCO and teachers, in consultation with the parents and pupil, must agree on the support to be provided to the pupil. There should also be a discussion about the intended impact of the support on the progress, development and or/behavior of the child. Dates will also be agreed in relation to when to review the support provided.

Do: Regardless of the support provided, the subject teacher will remain responsible for working with the child on a daily basis. The subject teacher should form a collaborative relationship with teaching assistant, SENCO and other key support staff to ensure that they are able to plan and assess the support provided.

Review: The effectiveness of the agreed support should be reviewed regularly in relation to the timeframes previously agreed. Focus should be on the impact of interventions on pupil progress, attainment and/or behaviour. Pupil and parent perspectives should again be sought as part of this review process. Adjustments should be made to the support and interventions provided as and when the teachers and SENCO deem it necessary. It is essential that parents are informed about any changes that are made in this respect.

Education, health and care plans

In some instances, pupils will demonstrate such significant difficulties in learning that the school may consider it impossible or inappropriate to conduct its full chosen assessment procedure. This may occur when the school decides that significant specialist intervention is required that is beyond that reasonably offered by schools. A EHC would not usually be the first step in providing support to pupils with SEND. It is expected that schools would conduct their own assessment and planning procedures, as outlined above, before requesting local authority support. A EHC plan should be aspirational and support the progress and attainment of pupils with SEND. It is important to note that parents and pupils over the age of 16 can also request a EHC assessment. Guidance can be found in the *Code of Practice* (DfE/DoH 2015).

From what has been discussed above, it should be obvious that you, as a teacher, have pivotal roles in the planning, delivering and reviewing of SEN Support in your school. The attainment targets and the *Code of Practice* are methods of looking at the whole child and how they respond to various situations, and not just their motor abilities. It is therefore looking at the process of how the child performs over time and not just at the end result. This again helps in building up the picture of the child with SEND, reviewing how it makes the child feel when they are successful and listening to comments on how well they performed.

Task 5.2   The four stages of the *Code of Practice*

Using the table below, review the four stages of the *Code of Practice*. First reflect on your understanding of the terms and stages, then second explore how you can ensure these needs are met as part of your teaching, learning and assessment strategies.

Aspects of the Code of Practice	What is your understanding of these aspects?	How can you ensure they are delivered?
Assess		
Plan		
Do		
Review		
EHC plan		

Human movement and children with SEND

Human movement has many dimensions; all children want to exploit the body's capacity for movement, and they thrive in any accomplishments they make. A young child uses movement as a means of learning about themselves and the physical world and, however trivial it might seem, to seek recognition and confirmation in an adult's eyes as well as to enjoy movement for its own sake. They experiment, apply and develop movement in many different ways and this provides a two-way channel of learning, both to find out about physical learning and to gain feedback on their particular accomplishments. Indeed, movement should not only be associated with, or isolated within, PE – it happens in a multitude of everyday situations.

A movement pattern is a definite arrangement of muscle actions required to achieve a desired outcome, for example, walking, throwing a ball or jumping in the air. The spatial and rhythmic components remain relatively constant and can be practised, and are essential to achieving the desired outcome. A movement pattern may be likened to a general template, which then becomes a basis for a number of specific skills. This transfer of skills is critical if learning is to take place. To be versatile in movement, children with SEND need the widest possible range of experiences with opportunities for frequent application and practice.

In order to ensure that any human movement is assessed fairly and consistently it is important for teachers to be accurate in any judgements they make (see Bailey 2001). Consequently, when assessing pupils with SEND in PE you need to ensure that your processes are valid, reliable, objective and practical.

Validity

This is where the teacher assesses accurately what is supposed to be assessed. The skills, knowledge and understanding have to match the learning objectives of a lesson or unit whilst also involving the use of reliable strategies to measure what is to be assessed. Children with SEND, for example, may struggle with the planning of movement sequences and not the execution of the skills, therefore the child may be hampered by not knowing what is occurring at particular points in time and consequently this needs to be taken into account.

Reliability

This should ensure consistency of measurement under the same conditions and it is important that the process is seen to be fair, so any teacher who makes an assessment would find the same result.

Objectivity

This is related to reliability in as much as the assessment should not reflect personal or institutional prejudices. This is where personal judgements and assumptions can creep in about specific children or how their conditions may impact on performance. It is therefore important to recognise this in order to minimise its impact on your judgements.

Practicality

Too many schemes of assessment are time consuming and take much-needed teaching and learning time away from PE lessons. Therefore, the teacher needs to find a practical blend between the demand for detailed assessment information and the practicality of the lesson.

Conclusion

The importance of assessment has been clearly supported by many writers (Newton and Bowler 2010; Piotrowski 2000). Assessment should focus upon what pupils learn and how well they learn it. This information then becomes the basis for future planning and provides teachers with vital information on their own performance as a teacher. Carroll (1994) implies that assessment always involves making a judgement. Assessment does not simply record what pupils have done in a lesson, but also makes some sort of qualitative statement as well. Whilst there is a wide choice of different assessment procedures, these need to be decided on the basis of the purpose for which the assessment is being undertaken. This may well mean employing different techniques for different assessment purposes.

The first role of assessment is to improve teaching and learning. Assessment can give feedback to children, which can help them progress, and also allows the teacher to evaluate their effectiveness by assessing how well the learning objectives have been achieved. Learning objectives are specific statements, which set out exactly what you want the children to learn. They form the intention or purpose of the lesson and are realised through the content selected and the learning experiences given to the pupils. Assessment can also indicate the nature and level of a child's achievement at specific points in their school life – for example, end of key stage attainment targets (DfE 2014a). Assessment can also be used for diagnostic purposes; this is especially important in detecting additional learning needs in particular areas. It can also help to identify strengths and weaknesses, which will inform planning and teaching.

It is hoped that in this chapter it has become apparent that learning and assessment go hand-in-hand. In other words, if we teach children a basic movement pattern it is necessary for the teacher to assess the child's ability to perform the task. If the task is shown to be meaningful to the child and will enhance their everyday lives, then the assessment and feedback become very important. This is imperative to all teachers if learning is to progress and movement patterns and motor skills are to develop.

Chapter 6

Teaching and learning strategies

Introduction and context

It is recognised that learning has physical, cognitive, social, and emotional dimensions. Consequently, teachers need to think about how to develop intellectual and mental representational skills alongside consideration of the social environment within which learning takes place and the individual needs of the child. Pupils with SEND, like their age-peers, learn in different ways and it is important to acknowledge that this is affected by relationships with teachers. Thus, in order for effective learning and engagement to take place, teachers need to have a sound grasp of a wide array of issues and concepts in order to maximise children's physical, social, intellectual and emotional development.

In beginning to examine children's educational development there are four basic elements that impact on learning – they are social contexts, knowledge, the curriculum, and psychological issues. In order to begin to address the needs of children with SEND and/or their age-peers it is vital that teachers have a thorough appreciation of the potential impact they can have on the success or otherwise of a child's learning and development. These can be described as follows:

- **Social contexts** look at the relationship between teaching and learning environments and the ideological thinking and philosophical approaches of the time such as the NC, school culture, local community contexts, and the individual needs of children.
- **Knowledge** has a significant impact on the types of teaching strategies used and pupils' development of their learning. For example, children have different levels of knowledge, understanding and needs, which should be accommodated within every lesson by the teacher.
- **The curriculum** directs the nature and content of the specific subjects and whole school approaches that are often required as part of a statutory educational process. However, this still requires teachers to make professional judgements on the interpretation of the curriculum, particularly in light of its increasing flexibility in PE in particular.

- **Psychological issues** refer to the wide and diverse range of theoretical approaches that can be applied to teaching and learning and the discussion and reflection that needs to be part of a teacher's professional role. Furthermore, this requires teachers to be aware of new theoretical approaches that may arise and be ready to trial and apply them as necessary.

Task 6.1   The four elements of teaching

Look at the four elements of teaching above and consider what these mean to you, and what strategies you would need to employ when working specifically with children with SEND in PE.

Understanding learning

According to Kyriacou (1986), learning is a change in behaviour as a result of being engaged in an educational experience. In order to consider how learning occurs in children, there are many theories that have been proposed. For example, Piaget (1962) argues that children pass through stages before they gain the ability to perceive reason and understand what is going on. As a result, it is suggested that children go through sequential stages of development and that their thinking is very different to that of adults. Thus, Piaget would argue that teachers need to recognise the various stages of educational development that children are at as well as recognise the differences in thinking that children will have to interpret particular learning situations.

In contrast, Vygotsky (1962) shares part of Piaget's views, but stresses the importance of activity as the fundamental basis for learning. A key element of Vygotsky's theory is based around what he refers to as the zone of proximal development, which focuses upon the gap between what children can know and do themselves, and what they need help to achieve. Consequently, it is argued that children can learn experientially through active learning on their own and with others, but at some stage they will need specialist help to progress their learning to a higher plane.

Bruner's (1971) theory of social learning offers another perspective in which cultural social experience is seen as vital to children's development. As a result, all learning according to Bruner needs to take place as part of a wider social experience. This emphasises, in particular, the potential of the teacher and the environment in making or breaking success and development. This is of particular relevance to children with SEND in PE who need teachers to adopt flexible approaches to learning and be ready to respond to the individual needs that they present with.

Teaching styles can be described as methods of learning and experiencing that are built from a strategy that also combines the individual behaviour of the teacher. A range of teaching styles and learning preferences can be employed, ranging from command styles (teacher-directed) through reciprocal teaching (children working together) to a variety of self-teaching styles where people learn independently (see Mosston and Ashworth 2001). This continuum of teaching styles (and the range and differences that comprise different styles) are critical to matching the pupil and teacher experience together to ensure a successful outcome. In contrast to teaching styles are learning preferences, which basically describe the manner in which people's brains store information. Consequently, there is a wide range of learning theories and the critical factor to consider in ensuring effective learning is that teachers adapt their styles to the needs of specific learners and groups.

Task 6.2   Theories of learning

Using the table below review your understanding of the theories of learning articulated by Piaget, Bruner and Vygotsky. You should look to develop your understanding of each theory and then relate it to children with SEND in PE.

The range of learning styles

There are many different ways to classify learning preferences, which fall into general categories of perceptual modality, information processing, and personality patterns. The categories represent the different ways in which teachers focus their attention on the learner and can be described as follows:

- **Perceptual modalities** define biologically based reactions to our physical environment and represent the way children most efficiently adopt information. Teachers should help children to learn their perception style so that they can seek out information in the format that they process it most directly.

Learning theory	Your understanding of the theory	What is the relationship of the theory to including children with SEND in PE?
Piaget		
Vygotsky		
Bruner		

- **Information processing** distinguishes between the way children sense, think, solve problems, and remember information. Each child will have a preferred, consistent, and distinct way of perceiving, organising, and retaining information and it is vital that teachers grasp the individual differences in order to aid learning.
- **Personality patterns** focus on attention, emotion, and values. By appreciating these differences teachers are able to predict the way children will react and feel about different situations.

Although there is a range of theories on learning preferences, they can be grouped into three sensory types: auditory, tactile and visual, from which most other styles can be seen as related extensions.

- **Auditory learners** learn through listening (which may have increased significance if a child has a visual impairment), verbal lectures, discussions, talking things through, and listening to what others have to say. Auditory learners interpret the underlying meanings of speech through listening to tone of voice, pitch, speed and other nuances.
- **Tactile/kinaesthetic learners** learn through moving, doing, and touching. These children learn best from a hands-on approach whereby they actively explore the physical world around them. They tend to find it hard to sit still for long periods and may become distracted by their need for activity and exploration.
- **Visual learners** learn through seeing (which is essential to children who may have learning difficulties or hearing impairments). These learners need to see the teacher's body language and facial expression to fully understand the content of a lesson. They tend to prefer sitting at the front of the classroom to avoid visual obstructions (e.g. people's heads). They may think in pictures and learn best from visual displays including diagrams, illustrated text books, overhead transparencies, videos, flip-charts and hand-outs.

Task 6.3   Sensory learning

Review your understanding of auditory, tactile/kinaesthetic and visual learners, and consider how you could use this knowledge when including children with SEND in PE.

In support of the three basic sensory types, Kolb's model of learning (1976, 2014) is based around four aspects of:

- **reflective observation** – helping children to gain meaning and orientation to the activity they are going to participate in;
- **abstract conceptualisation** – giving children orientation to the theoretical concepts which underpin the activity;
- **concrete experience** – helping children towards solution-oriented experiences;
- **active experimentation** – in which children are oriented towards the activity in order to experience and learn from this.

In analysing Kolb's model of learning, there is a clear process of children moving through stages of observation, understanding concepts, looking for solutions, then experimenting through practice to learn and develop. For some children with SEND, particular stages may have more meaning and emphasis than others and this needs to be taken into account by the teacher. For example, a child with a visual impairment will not rely so much on reflective observation, but will need to have further support with understanding the physical movement concepts that are required to perform a particular skill. Consequently, the key to successful learning experiences lies in the ability of the teacher to recognise how children learn best in relation to their needs.

Gardiner's theory of learning styles (1988)

In addition to the work of Kolb, Gardiner's learning styles are based around what is often described as multiple intelligences based upon identifying seven different ways of children demonstrating their intellectual ability. This, again, is a key focus for teachers to consider, particularly when working with children with SEND as part of them demonstrating their knowledge and understanding of a subject in a manner which suits their specific needs. The seven styles are as follows:

- **Verbal and/or linguistic intelligence** is concerned with the ability to use words and language. These learners have highly developed auditory skills and are generally articulate speakers. They tend to think in words rather than pictures and their skills include listening, speaking, writing, storytelling, explaining, using humour, understanding the syntax and meaning of words, remembering information, convincing someone of their point of view, and analysing language usage.
- **Mathematical intelligence** is concerned with the ability to use reason, logic, and numbers. These children think conceptually in logical and numerical patterns, making connections between pieces of information, and are always curious about the world around them. In addition, they tend to ask lots of questions and like to do experiments. Their skills include problem solving, classifying and categorising information, working with abstract concepts to figure out the relationship of each to the other, handling long chains of

reason to make local progressions, doing controlled experiments, questioning and wondering about natural events, performing complex mathematical calculations, and working with geometric shapes.

- **Visual/spatial intelligence** refers to the ability to perceive visual images, and these children tend to think in pictures and need to create vivid mental images to retain information. They enjoy looking at maps, charts, pictures, videos, and movies, and their skills include puzzle building, reading, writing, understanding charts and graphs, sense of direction, sketching, painting, creating visual metaphors and analogies (perhaps through the visual arts), manipulating images, constructing, fixing, designing practical objects, and interpreting visual images.

- **Bodily/kinaesthetic intelligence** refers to the ability to control body movements and handle objects skilfully. These learners express themselves through movement and have a good sense of balance and hand–eye coordination (for example, ball play, balancing beams). Through interacting with the space around them, they are able to remember and process information, and their skills include dancing, physical co-ordination, sport, hands-on experimentation, using body language, crafts, acting, miming, using their hands to create or build, and expressing emotions through the body.

- **Musical/rhythmic intelligence** refers to the ability to produce and appreciate music and these children are often inclined to think in sounds, rhythms, and patterns. They immediately respond to music, either by appreciating or criticising what they hear, with many of the learners being extremely sensitive to environmental sounds. Their skills are focused upon singing, whistling, playing musical instruments, recognising tonal patterns, composing music, remembering melodies and understanding the structure and rhythm of music.

- **Interpersonal intelligence** relates to an ability to relate to and understand others, with such children trying to see things from other people's point of view in order to understand how they think and feel. They often have the ability to sense feelings, intentions, and motivations, and are great organisers, although they sometimes resort to manipulation. Generally, they try to maintain peace in group settings and encourage co-operation whilst using both verbal (for example, speaking) and non-verbal (for example, eye contact, body language) language to open communication channels with others. Their skills include seeing things from other perspectives (dual-perspective), listening, using empathy, understanding other people's moods and feelings, counselling, co-operating with groups, noticing people's moods, motivations and intentions, communicating both verbally and non-verbally, building trust, peaceful conflict resolution, and establishing positive relations with other people.

- **Intrapersonal intelligence** refers to the ability to self-reflect and be aware of one's inner state of being. These learners try to understand their inner feelings, dreams, relationships with others, and strengths and weaknesses.

Their skills include recognising their own strengths and weaknesses, reflecting and analysing themselves, awareness of their inner feelings, desires and dreams, evaluating their thinking patterns, reasoning with themselves, and understanding their role in relationship to others.

In summary, by teachers having an appreciation of the variety of intelligences that children may demonstrate it offers the potential for children to maximise their learning and development whilst giving them the best opportunities to demonstrate and gain knowledge and understanding in PE. This is critical with children with SEND, who may have particular intelligences which teachers can work through in order to tap into their learning behaviour and activities.

Teaching and learning in the context of children with SEND in PE

All teachers have their own teaching styles, which are part of the diversity of PE experiences that can be presented to children with SEND. However, what is more important than an individual teacher's particular style of delivery is the ability to demonstrate a comprehensive range of teaching, learning and assessment strategies in order to be able to adapt and modify practice according to individual needs and specific class, activity or environmental needs. Thus, as we have the potential to teach in different ways, so children need to learn in different ways. This section of the chapter sets out to provide you with a range of teaching and learning strategies that you may wish to consider as part of the enhancement of your inclusive PE practice. In fact, it is important to recognise that if we as teachers can get better at delivering a range of teaching styles it will benefit all children, and not just those with SEND.

PE has a distinctive role to play with children with SEND, as it does not just focus on the education of the physical, but it also has social, emotional, cognitive, moral and language dimensions as well. Consequently, a first step in the teaching and learning process is to consider the learning outcomes of the PE lesson. These could possibly be split into two categories, which focus upon principles of learning to move and moving to learn, which both have desirable outcomes for a child with SEND in PE.

Learning to move is an intrinsic benefit of PE and can be seen as the traditional outcome of a lesson. This is where teachers identify skills to be taught and learned by the pupils in a variety of contexts. This may have a particular focus if a child has movement difficulties in PE, and outcomes may be modified to accommodate this need.

Moving to learn is where outcomes are based more on the result of experiences rather than a focus on the quality of movement and/or specific physical skills. This can be described as more of an extrinsic benefit and PE offers many opportunities for developing pupils' co-operation, empathy, teamwork, leadership skills and so on. The objectives here tend to be more immediate and can be very specific to an individual child's needs. For example, if a child needs to learn how to take turns or listen to the views of others, this can be set up as a specific outcome for the child to work on. This will naturally have wider social benefits than the PE context if, for instance, a child learns to be more accommodating with their behaviour when with others.

Task 6.4   Learning to move, and moving to learn

Read again the descriptors related to the concepts of learning to move, and moving to learn. Use the table below to summarise a range of strategies that would accommodate this type of learning outcome in PE lessons.

Planning and delivering your teaching and learning

The issues related to the planning, organisation, delivery, and review of your teaching and learning in many ways are just the same for children with SEND as they are for other children. Consequently, if we are to make attempts at improving our mixed ability teaching this will benefit all pupils within our classes and potentially make us better teachers. The distinction comes, however, in the specific nature of how you as the teacher can address the individual needs of children with SEND. It is often the case that only minor changes to your teaching, learning and assessment will be required to accommodate children with SEND in order for them to gain their full entitlement and accessibility to the PE curriculum. However, the question that is often posed is, where do I start in considering the needs of children with SEND in PE? A good starting point is to make a list of what information and issues you are likely to need to know about in order to address the needs of specific children within specific activity and environmental contexts. This list could include ensuring that as part of your planning you have:

- collected up-to-date medical information;
- consulted with teachers, parents, and pupils;
- established class routines;
- read individual education plans and/or education, health and care plans;
- been open to modification of teaching and learning outcomes;
- considered assessment strategies.

Objective	Strategies to employ to meet the specific context within which learning will take place
Learning to move Moving to learn	

Grouping and support in the PE lesson

A central issue to the success or otherwise of your PE lesson and the experience gained by the child is that you have taken into account the grouping and support that may be required in particular contexts. Thus, you will need to carefully consider each part of the lesson plan and organisation, and anticipate whether children are best working individually, reciprocally and/or in large groups. If you consider these issues in advance it can make a major difference in the success of your learning activity, whilst constantly bearing in mind the need to still be flexible and open to modifying activities as you progress through them.

It is worth considering that in any typical PE class you will have children who are on a diverse continuum of learning needs. Consequently, groups need to be carefully matched according to their confidence and skill level, and the nature of the activity being delivered. It is important to remember, however, that it is not necessary always to group people according to physical ability. There are many examples in which a child who struggles with physical competence can be paired with someone who is more careful and both can be equally stretched and receive their full entitlement to the curriculum. For example, a child with cerebral palsy who may struggle to send and receive a ball could be paired with a competent ball-thrower. The proficient ball- thrower will have to work on precision, accuracy and weighting of the ball to ensure the other child has the best success in receiving the ball, whilst the variety of sending that may be returned by the child with cerebral palsy will help the proficient child to be adaptable to changing sending patterns.

In other PE contexts it may, however, be more advantageous to pair pupils of similar ability together. This would be the case in gymnastic or dance activities where, if they are working on sequencing or mirroring work, the pupils will be working at a similar level to each other. Other grouping contexts, such as competitive activities, need to be given careful consideration. When pupils are working on small-scale skill development they often work well and function at their own levels. However, in large group settings difference often presents itself at the most extreme. As a result, it may be better to group people who are at similar physical and emotional levels, or work specifically on ensuring that all team members have a role to play that is appropriate to their needs.

Task 6.5   Grouping pupils

Reflect upon the comments in relation to grouping pupils and consider what issues and challenges you may face when dealing with children who are working on a diverse continuum of learning needs.

If a child has a EHC plan there may or may not be an element of learning assistant support available, but this will depend on the individual needs and circumstances of the child and school context. It is important, though, to ensure that if you feel support is required you discuss this with the SENCO to work out strategies for accommodating any particular support arrangements. Whilst a learning support assistant is there to help the child, it is important to recognise that you are still responsible for the planning, organisation, and delivery of that child's PE lesson. Consequently, you are responsible for guiding and working with the support assistant to ensure the child gets the best experience possible. It is also important to recognise that often the support assistant will spend the majority of the day with one child and will be a valuable resource to you in developing your planning and organisation. See Chapter 7 for a more detailed discussion about working with learning support assistants and SENCOs.

In addition to the support of a learning assistant, there are many other methods of support that a child with SEND may need. These may include:

- help in breaking down tasks to smaller constituent parts to aid explanation and understanding;
- providing specific feedback to pupils with particular contexts (particularly if the child has learning difficulties, or sensory needs);
- physical support if a child has restricted ranges of movement;
- repeating instructions and offering further guidance in order to make it more meaningful;
- adapting the nature of the outcomes or activity (for example changes to rules, equipment and so on).

Developing strategies for task adaptation

Changing the nature of the task to accommodate individual children with SEND requires careful thought and planning in order to be effective. This may involve changes to rules, equipment, tasks and the like in order to ensure full accessibility to the activity. This may not mean significant changes to the task, and you often will find that only minor modifications will make a substantial difference to the accessibility and entitlement that child receives. For example, offering children a selection of different ball sizes or equipment with shorter or longer handles often results in them naturally selecting the equipment they are most comfortable with. Furthermore, you can change the rules to ensure some pupils have more time on the ball or all have to receive a pass before scoring. Placing pupils into their own zones and territories is another method of adapting the task to accommodate different needs.

The most important issue to bear in mind when adapting tasks is that you ensure that:

- any modification and adaptation to the task does not affect its integrity and is not patronising or tokenistic;
- accessibility to the PE lessons remains the responsibility of the teacher, in consultation with support assistants and pupils where necessary;
- any modifications to an activity do not affect its curriculum relevance;
- any modification to small-sided or modified activities should be planned with the intention of moving to the full activity and with the use of full equipment if possible;
- children have an entitlement to access the PE curriculum and it is the school's responsibility to deliver this.

An important aspect of planning work with children with SEND is the need to consider the most appropriate methods of breaking the tasks down to smaller constituent parts. Here, the teacher will need to consider the child's physical, intellectual, emotional and social needs as part of the organisation and development of activities. As a result, in order for the child to progress, careful consideration of what stage each pupil's learning and development is at is essential if meaningful and successful participation is to take place. Part of this will require some consultation with the child in order that they know what is being expected of them.

Task 6.6   Adapting tasks

Look at the issues around adapting tasks discussed above. Using the table below, consider how you would ensure you address these issues within your teaching and learning activity with children with SEND.

Guidelines to inclusive teaching and learning approaches

Whilst there are no definitive protocols to follow when planning, organising and delivering inclusive PE there are certain fundamental principles that will help you develop entitlement and accessibility in your lessons. Applying these principles will act as a focus for your reflection in ensuring that any differentiated

Aspect of adaptation	Strategies to ensure delivery
Maintaining integrity	
Accessibility is the responsibility of the teacher	
Keeping activities relevant to the curriculum	
Ensuring entitlement to the PE curriculum	

practices also offer integrity, which is vital to enabling children to feel comfortable and confident in their PE experiences. These include:

- **organisational adaptations** such as the physical location of the learning environment – this is of particular importance if you are working with children with mobility needs, where physical accessibility may be a particular problem;
- **support arrangements** before, during and after the lesson;
- **grouping and organisation** of pupils within the lessons according to individual need and learning context;
- **variety** of **teaching styles,** involving a readiness to change and adapt to meet the needs of individual learners;
- **attention to the breaking down of tasks** to ensure children have a clear awareness of and guidance on what is being expected of them;
- **differentiated assessment strategies** that act to prevent barriers to children demonstrating their knowledge, understanding, and learning to date;
- **matching the activity** to the levels of children in order to ensure learning and development;
- **modification to equipment** including rules, equipment, height, colours, weights, and textures of resources;
- **modifications to space** including the use of zoning.

Conclusion

The development of effective teaching, learning and assessment strategies is critical for the effective inclusion of children with SEND in PE. As part of creating effective processes, teachers need to be committed to developing flexibility in their pedagogical practices whilst responding positively to the need to modify and adapt strategies and style to meet the needs of individual learners. A central aspect of this comes through recognition of social models of disability, in which it is the teacher's and school's responsibility to change what they are doing to accommodate children with SEND, rather than the other way round.

Chapter 7

Multi-disciplinary approaches and working in partnership

Introduction and context

The 1997 government report *Excellence for All Children* (DfEE 1997a) highlighted a need to improve the consistency of SEND provision across the country, so that every child gets the best education available, regardless of where they live. Regional partnerships can contribute to making this happen by helping local authorities and other providers work together so they can share experience and knowledge and, where possible, plan and develop services as a region, rather than individually. The need for agencies and individuals to work in partnership through multi-disciplinary approaches is a vital element in ensuring that children with SEND and their teachers receive the best support, advice and guidance required to produce successful learning and participation.

Regional partnerships can help resolve the problem of variations in SEND services across the country, so that the services available to children do not depend on where they live. One of the main ways of doing this is to bring together all those involved in SEND in a particular region, so they can share expertise and experience, learn from each other's successes, identify gaps in provision, and plan how to fill them.

By promoting this regional approach to planning and provision, the partnerships can help to make sure that:

- the right SEND services are available to those who need them;
- services are provided as efficiently as possible;
- examples of best practice can be learned from and extended;
- Local and regional expertise is being used to inform central government policy making.

If agencies outside of school and individual practitioners within schools work together to support the educational development of children with SEND through holistic approaches this will contribute to aiding their social, physical, emotional and intellectual needs both within and outside of school. This chapter sets out to examine the roles that some professionals play in supporting teachers and children with SEND and to state the case for working in partnership rather than in isolation as a means to successful and meaningful participation and engagement in PE.

Task 7.1   Multi-agency working

Review what you see as the advantages and potential disadvantages and challenges of taking a multi-disciplinary partnership approach to the inclusion of children with SEND in PE.

Defining partnerships

Partnerships can be described as arrangements between two or more parties who have agreed to work co-operatively towards shared and/or compatible objectives and in which there is shared authority and responsibility; joint investment of resources; shared liability or risk-taking; and, ideally, mutual benefits. Taken together, these definitions suggest the following four key elements, which distinguish and define partnerships:

- common objectives and goals among partners (objectives may be the impetus of the partnership or they may evolve over time);
- shared risk and mutual benefits (risks and benefits may be different for each partner and may accrue with different timeframes);
- contributions from both partners (including both monetary and nonmonetary);
- shared authority, responsibility and accountability.

Underlying many of these definitions is also the notion that the partnership represents, to all partners, a better strategy to address a specific project or goal than each partner operating independently. In other words, the partnership is considered to add value to the efforts of the individual partners. This is certainly the case when working with children with SEND, who may have a range of needs that have to be addressed. Consequently, a central feature of successful inclusion is the commitment and desire for multi-agency and partnership working approaches. For example, a child who has restricted ranges of movement may well need the services of a physiotherapist who can support the child with extending and developing physical activity safely. As a result, the lesson can support any remedial work that is done, but at the same time physiotherapy should not be seen as a replacement for PE. Children still need and deserve their entitlement to the activities of the PE NC, and working with physiotherapists within the curriculum can only aid school and wider lifestyle experience and involvement.

The strategic involvement of education, health, and care partners

The Children and Families Act places a legal duty on local authorities (LAs) to develop, maintain and utilise a strategic partnership with education, health, and social care in order to promote wellbeing and improve the quality of provision provided to children with SEND. In this respect, LAs and clinical commissioning groups (CCGs) must make joint commissioning arrangements for education, health, and care provision for children and young people with SEND. There is flexibility in relation to who the local authority engages as strategic partners. However, according to the *Code of Practice* (DfE/DoH 2015), joint commissioning arrangements must cover the services for children both with and without EHC plans. These services are to include, but not be limited to:

- specialist support and therapies, such as clinical treatments and delivery of medications;
- speech and language therapy;
- assistive technology;
- personal care (or access to it);
- Child and Adolescent Mental Health Services (CAMHS) support;
- occupational therapy;
- rehabilitation training;
- physiotherapy;
- a range of nursing support; and
- specialist equipment, wheelchairs, and continence supplies and also emergency provision.

Health services should help with the early identification, assessment, and provision for children with SEND to support to ensure that conditions such as chronic fatigue syndrome and anxiety disorders are understood by teachers and appropriately catered for during the planning and delivery of PE lessons. Community paediatricians in conjunction with other health professionals, particularly therapists, are often the first people to identify a SEND and notify local authorities. They also provide diagnostic services and health reports for EHC needs assessments (DfE/DoH 2015). Where a child or young person has been assessed as having social care needs in relation to their SEND, social care teams:

- must secure social care provision under the Chronically Sick and Disabled Persons Act (CSDPA) 1970, which has been assessed as being necessary to support a child or young person's SEND and which is specified in their EHC plan;

- should provide early years providers, schools and colleges with a contact for social care advice on children and young people with SEND;
- must undertake reviews of children and young people with EHC plans where there are social care needs; and
- should make sure that for looked after children and care leavers the arrangements for assessing and meeting their needs across education, health and social care are co-ordinated effectively within the process of care and pathway planning, in order to avoid duplication and delay.

(DfE/DoH 2015: 51)

Task 7.2   Partnership approaches to SEND in PE

Using the table below, review your understanding of the roles of health, education and social services in terms of what services, advice and guidance they can offer to each other and what the benefits are likely to be to you as the teacher and the child with SEND.

Holistic approaches and the role of specialists

One of the central components of successful inclusion is the ability of a wide range of professionals to work together to provide a co-ordinated support service to specific children with SEND. In relation to PE, taking a holistic approach to children with SEND is vital if teachers are to be aware of all the needs and issues that may face them, and have the resources, information and guidance to be in a position to take appropriate action. As a result, the types of support teachers are likely to need when supporting children with SEND in PE are those from specialists such as physiotherapists, occupational therapists, educational psychologists, nurses, speech and language therapists and sometimes disability governing bodies of sport. In drawing together this multi-disciplinary team of professionals, the knowledge and understanding that can be gained by teachers

Authority	What is your understanding of the role of each agency?	What are the benefits of collaborative working for the teacher of children with SEND in PE?
Social services		
Health authorities		
Education authorities		

in order to give a comprehensive understanding of child with SEND is critical. Furthermore, teachers will help to ensure that they provide a co-ordinated and whole-person centred approach to the specific needs of children, by listening to and reflecting upon the advice and guidance given by each professional.

In relation to the role of occupational therapists, in order for them to qualify and practise they are required to have a thorough appreciation of aspects of anatomy, physiology, neurology, and psychology in order to assist with the assessment and support of children with functional difficulties. These therapists are primarily of use to teachers and children in that they have specific skills in observation and activity analysis and the implementation of carefully graded activities to develop, learn or re-learn skills to foster independent living. Furthermore, and with specific relevance to supporting children with SEND in PE, paediatric occupational therapists' knowledge of neurology, child development, and cognitive psychology offers teachers an insight into the understanding of gross and fine motor skills and movement in order to help them plan effective educational programmes.

In contrast, physiotherapists have knowledge and appreciation of anatomy and physiology, and are experts in analysing movement. They are particularly focused around aspects of the examination of children's movement based on the structure and function of the body and physical approaches to promoting health, preventing injury, treatment and rehabilitation, and the management of particular disability conditions. Consequently, in relation to supporting children with SEND in PE, physiotherapists can help teachers to improve the quality and ranges of movement that are central to successful learning and participation.

Speech and language therapists offer essential information in helping children who have speech errors and communication and language development issues. They are of particular importance to teachers of PE in helping them to ensure children are able to communicate and interact in effective ways with their peers and tutors. In addition, teachers can, through PE, reinforce any particular language programmes that are being worked on with a child with SEND.

Educational psychologists focus on the study of learning outcomes, student attributes, and instructional processes that directly relate to the classroom and the school. In addition, they can support pupils and teachers in ensuring that individual needs are clearly understood, then plan for effective and supportive educational programmes. As part of the statutory assessment of SEND under the *Code of Practice,* an educational psychologist helps gather information for teachers, parents, and professional support agencies. They also assist in evaluating children's thinking abilities and assessing individual strengths and weaknesses. Together, the parents, teachers, and educational psychologist formulate plans to help children learn more effectively and are critical to the co-ordinated and multi-disciplinary partnership approaches to the support of children with SEND in PE.

Task 7.3   The role of therapists

Using the table below, outline in your own words what you see as the different roles therapists play in supporting children with SEND. You should then relate this specifically to how these therapists can support you as a teacher to ensure you have a full grasp of the individual needs of children with SEND and how they relate to PE.

Working with special educational needs coordinators and learning support assistants

As well as drawing on the expertise of professionals external to the school, it is also extremely important that all those who are a part of schools work together to facilitate the inclusion of children with SEND. For PE teachers, special educational needs coordinators (SENCOs) and learning support assistants (LSAs) can provide the crucial support needed to achieve the full inclusion of all their pupils. It was the 1994 SEN *Code of Practice* that established the role of SENCO. A SENCO is an educational specialist whose remit was to liaise with and advising teachers, parents, senior leadership team (SLT) and external agencies vis-à-vis challenges and potential solutions to including children with SEND in mainstream schools. They were also charged with the task of inclusion training of staff, managing LSAs, assessing pupils with SEND, and managing the records and statements of pupils with SEND (DoE 1994).

In small schools (i.e. those with fewer pupils and staff) the head teacher or deputy may take on this role, whereas in larger schools there may be a SEND coordinating team or even department. In short, the role of SENCO was created and is maintained to ensure that an inclusive culture develops in schools. Given changes to *Codes of Practice*, among other things, the role of SENCO has developed and changed over time and space. With a greater devolution of power to schools generally, and senior leaders in school in particular, the role, responsibilities and influence a SENCO has can differ from school to school. Below, we outline some of the main responsibilities of SENCOs, and explore how you, as a teacher, can work with SENCOs to ensure that your pupils have meaningful experiences of PE.

Therapist	Your understanding of their role	How can these therapists support teachers in PE?
Occupational therapists		
Physiotherapist		
Speech and language therapist		
Educational psychologist		

Whilst LSAs have formed an integral part of some schools in Britain ever since the Plowden Report in 1967 (Central Advisory Council for Education 1967), they gained much more political and academic attention nearly 35 years later after the British Government announced that schools of the future would include many more trained staff to support learning to higher standards (Morris 2001) through facilitating the inclusion of pupils with SEND. The Department for Education and Skills (2001) identified four key strands to the role of LSA: (1) supporting pupils; (2) supporting teachers; (3) supporting the school; and (4) supporting the curriculum. It is clear that LSAs are employed in an auxiliary capacity in schools but it is not clear what their role, specifically, should and does entail. The remainder of this chapter will draw on Government policy and academic literature to explore how schools operationalise LSAs, and how PE teachers can work with LSAs to ensure that they are fulfilling their legal requirement to ensure that pupils with SEND are included in their lessons.

Task 7.4 The role of SENCOs

Using the table below, consider your understanding of the proposed roles of SENCOs and explore the ways in which these roles can support you in your attempts to include pupils with SEND in PE.

Task 7.5 The role of LSAs

Similarly, use the table below and consider your understanding of the proposed roles of LSAs and explore the ways in which these roles can support you in your endeavours to include children with SEND in PE.

Role of SENCO	Your understanding of their role	How it may support your attempts to be inclusive in PE
Advise teachers, parents, and SLT		
Staff inclusion training		
Managing LSAs		
Assessing pupils with SEND		
Managing SEND information		

Role of LSA	Your understanding of their role	How it may support your attempts to be inclusive in PE
Supporting pupils		
Supporting teachers		
Supporting schools		
Supporting the curriculum		

According to Cowne (2005: 67), 'the modern SENCO has to be master of many trades', because of the wide and diverse nature of SEND policy, processes, and practice nationally and in schools in particular. It is the SENCO who is expected to oversee the day-to-day operation of the school's SEND policy. SEND policies can vary across schools but all will align with the legal requirements laid out in the *Code of Practice* (DfE/DoH 2015). It is the role of the SENCO to ensure that the school's SEN policy reflect any changes in government policy, and that subject teachers, such as yourself, are aware of the policy and that it underpins what you do in practice. With this in mind, we would encourage you to read your school's SEN policy and discuss with the SENCO what this means for you. This is an easy, practical way, of developing that relationship with the SENCO that is so important for your endeavours to be an inclusive teacher.

As mentioned previously, the SENCO is also responsible for assessing SEND. Teachers play an extremely important role in this process because they are the ones who spend the most time with pupils in school and, therefore, are most aware of their learning needs and capabilities. Given that research suggests that much of the SEND information and provision in schools relates mostly to classroom-based subjects (Maher 2013), it is essential that PE teachers work closely with SENCOs to ensure that assessment procedures are relevant to PE, and that any provision developed reflects the fact that corporeal practices are a part of PE. In this respect, it is important to remember that it is you who is the subject expert, not the SENCO. Therefore, your knowledge of PE pedagogy and content will be crucial for the development of suitable provision and learning targets.

SENCOs also provide the bridge between the school and organisations external to the school such as the local authority, educational psychologists, and health and care professionals, as discussed above. Often, the external professionals will, to varying degrees, support the delivery of PE through providing expert advice and services, such as physiotherapy for children who require it. This creates opportunities for PE teachers to upskill themselves by learning from professionals with different, but relevant, skills and expertise.

SENCOs as part of the senior leadership team

Mainstream schools have a legal duty to identify an experienced teacher as its SENCO. The government also 'recommends' that SENCOs are part of the

SLT (DfE/DoH 2015). This will help ensure that 'inclusion' is at the heart of discussions by those in key decision making position within a school. It should also mean that there is at least one member of staff 'championing' inclusion and children with SEND when school-wide and subjects-specific decisions are being made about resourcing, financing and developments associated with curriculum and pedagogy.

It is essential, therefore, that PE teachers develop a strong and collaborative relationship with SENCOs to ensure their subject-specific concerns and achievements are part of those discussions. Not only should inclusion be at the heart of discussions by those in key decision-making positions, but PE too. This may go some way to redressing a significant imbalance when it comes to subject priorities in schools where PE was found to rank 9th out of 11 subjects when it came to the development of SEND provision and distribution of SEND resources across curriculum areas (Maher and Macbeth 2013). This is problematic because a lack of SEND provision and resources can constrain the extent to which teachers are able to provide meaningful PE experiences to pupils with SEND.

In this respect, it is important to note that not all SENCOs are part of the SLT. The decision whether to make SENCOs part of SLT resides with senior leaders within each school. SENCOs who are part of the SLT find it extremely beneficial because they are able to ensure that inclusion and the experiences of children with SEND are at the heart of school development activities and whole-school strategic planning (Maher and Vickerman 2018). In addition, they report to have more influence over curriculum interventions and have more time to liaise with colleagues such as subject teachers (Szwed 2007).

For those who are not a part of SLT, they find it more difficult to coordinate whole-school developments. For instance, many of the SENCOs in a study conducted by Weddell (2004) suggested that, because they were not a member of the SLT, they were rarely allowed to manage the SEND budget and, as a result, were unaware of how much money was allocated to SEND in their school. In many instances, it is a head of finance who is making these budgetary decisions rather than the SENCO. This is potentially problematic given that they are not an inclusion or pedagogy expert. Therefore, they will be less aware of the specific SEND needs and requirements of pupils, subject areas and the school more generally.

The importance of PE teachers developing strong, collaborative relationships with SENCOs becomes perhaps even more apparent when considered in relation to the views of PE teachers in research conducted by Morley et al. (2005), who suggested that they were often neglected by SENCOs. Whether this neglect is actual or perceived is difficult to say. What can be said is that SENCOs are the inclusion experts within a school, therefore their knowledge, skills and experiences will be extremely useful for PE teachers who teach pupils with SEND in PE.

> ## Task 7.6   Your relationship with the SENCO
>
> Reflect on your current working relationship with your SENCO. Use the table below to consider how it could be improved to benefit both parties.

The training of SENCOs for inclusion (in PE)

Appropriate training is important for SENCOs, like teachers, to ensure that they have the knowledge, skills and relevant experiences to fulfil the full remit of their role. Since 2009, SENCOs new to the role must hold 'The National Award for Special Educational Needs Coordination' (DfE/DoH 2015). The courses that confer this award are delivered by universities and specific content and focus can differ across higher education institutions. However, all are mapped against the national award for special educational needs coordination (NCTL 2014). The learning outcomes for the award as set out by the National College for Teaching and Leadership, and reflect the diverse role and responsibilities of the SENCO as outlined above. These learning outcomes relate to the following:

- the professional knowledge and understanding that SENCOs need of the legislative context for SEND and theoretical concepts that underpin effective leadership and practice;
- the expertise and capabilities that SENCOs need to lead and coordinate provision effectively;
- the personal and professional qualities that SENCOs need to make a positive impact on the ethos and culture in schools and other setting.

(NCTL 2014: 5)

There is an ever-growing body of research that has attempted to explore the impact of the National Award on the leadership, whole-school strategies for removing barriers to inclusion, and the pedagogies of SENCOs. Brown and Doveston (2014) suggest that the National Award has impacted positively on the pedagogies of SENCOs and their ability to remove barrier to inclusion for children with SEND. A lack of time and status within the school hierarchy, however, were identified as constraining the extent to which the knowledge

---

What does your current relationship with the SENCO involve?
How does this help you with your attempts to be inclusive in PE?
How is this relationship beneficial to the SENCO?
*What could you do to improve this relationship to benefit both parties
    but, more importantly, the children you teach?*

and skills developed during the National Award could be used in schools (Brown and Doveston 2014).

Maher and Macbeth (2013) are two of a few academics who have explored the usefulness of SENCO training for facilitating the inclusion of children with SEND in PE. Their research, which was from the perspective of SENCOs themselves, suggested that SENCOs had not received any PE-specific training, nor any training they though especially relevant to PE. This is potentially problematic given that corporeal practices in PE, which occur within learning environments very different from classroom-based subjects, create challenges to inclusion that many other subject teachers do not experience. This, coupled with the fact that SEND is contextual (can differ across subjects) and situational (can differ across learning activities), has resulted in Maher and Macbeth (2013) arguing that SENCOs should receive some PE-specific training.

Given the significant financial constraints placed on local authorities and schools, it is very unlikely that this will happen anytime soon. Thus, it is perhaps even more important that PE teachers and SENCOs work closely together. SENCOs are said to be the inclusion experts; teachers are said to be the subject experts. Therefore, a collaborative approach is required to explore how EHC plans, for example, which contain generic information, can be translated and applied to PE. This is but one example of how PE teachers and SENCOs can work together to support each other and, more importantly, children with SEND in PE.

Task 7.7 SENCO training

Consider the training undertaken by SENCOs through the National Award. Use the table below to explore the ways in which this training can be useful for supporting you and your pupils in PE.

Training focus	How could it be utilised to support you and your pupils?
Professional knowledge and understanding of the legislative context for SEND	
Theoretical concepts that underpin effective leadership and practice	
The expertise and capabilities needed to lead and coordinate SEND provision effectively	
The personal and professional qualities needed to make a positive impact on the inclusive ethos and inclusive culture of your school	

The management of LSAs

Under the previous *Code of Practice* (DfES 2001b), SENCOs were responsible, if only partly, for the recruitment, training and deployment of LSAs. Many of these duties, however, have mostly been taken away from SENCOs, although aspects remain depending on the school in which you work. Recruitment and deployment especially now seems to be within the remit of senior leadership teams within schools, with SENCOs only having influence over who is employed and what they do if they are part of SLT (Maher and Macbeth 2013; Maher and Vickerman 2018).

However, research conducted by Szwed (2007) suggested that, in practice, it is often unclear who is managing, working with, or supporting LSAs. More often than not, these responsibilities are divided, not necessarily uniformly, amongst SENCOs, SLT, and the subject teachers themselves. This approach could potentially lead to confusion due to a lack of coherence and communication within and between schools (Szwed 2007). Maher and Macbeth (2013) have argued that one potential outcome of such inconsistent and incoherent support mechanism in some schools could be that some pupils with SEND will not get the support that their specific needs require. For you as a teacher, then, it is important to know the specific role(s) of the LSAs that support your lessons and what is expected of you in relation to their deployment and usage.

LSAs as facilitators of inclusion in PE

The specific functions of LSAs can differ significantly within and across schools. All, however, are a crucial support mechanism that can help to facilitate the inclusion of pupils with SEND in all subjects, including PE. According to LSAs themselves, they work in schools to support children and facilitate learning (Maher and Vickerman 2018). Interestingly, this view differed from the perspective offered by SENCOs, who argued that LSAs are there to support teachers to delivered curriculum content (Maher and Vickerman 2018). There is an important distinction to be made here in that the ultimate focus should be on pupils learning rather than teachers teaching, and one way in which this can be achieved is through LSAs supporting teachers to teach; the teaching is the 'means' and the learning is the 'end'.

There is an ever-growing body of literature that has attempted to analyse the impact of LSAs on pupils and schools. For example, a report by Reform, an independent non-party think tank, suggests that LSAs have little impact on educational outcomes (Bassett et al. 2010). It is important to note, however, that this outcome-orientated way of measuring impact is tied to performance criteria relating to the cognitive domain of learning. Little is said, here, about the physical, social and affective domains, to which LSAs can also contribute.

On a more pragmatic level, research conducted by Alborz et al. (2009) suggests that LSAs enable teachers to spend more time working with small groups and individuals, which can result in the teacher feeling supported and under less stress. However, it must be remembered that LSAs are not qualified teachers. Therefore, they should not be teaching pupils; more, LSAs should be facilitating the learning of pupils with SEND as they are taught by you, the person who is qualified to do so.

Another limitation of an LSA being assigned to a single pupil – known as the Velcro model (Gerschel 2005) – is the potential for a culture of dependency: the pupil may become emotionally, physically, and socially dependent on the LSA, which may result in the pupil becoming isolated from their age-peers. Indeed, there is research from the perspective of pupils with SEND in PE that suggests that LSAs can create a social barrier between pupils with and without SEND (Fitzgerald 2005), which is particularly problematic given that pupils with SEND in research conducted by Atkinson and Black (2006) considered the social element of PE as being the most important reason for taking part.

On the other hand, Gerschel (2005) suggests that when pupils and LSAs are rotated, some of the more vulnerable pupils are not sure who to turn to when they required advice and support because there are different support staff in different lessons. The study also suggests that the rotation system meant that no single LSA had an overview of each pupil's progress as far as support was concerned, which could be problematic (Gerschel 2005). Therefore, it is important that teachers and LSA strike an adequate balance when it comes to the amount and type of support and autonomy they give pupils with SEND. This, of course, will depend on the needs and capabilities of the pupil, and should be part of a broader discussion between teacher, LSA, SENCO, parents and, where appropriate, pupil. It is also important that these decisions are reviewed regularly. Remember, the onus is on you, the subject teacher, to have a detailed understanding of the needs and capabilities of pupils with SEND, and their support requirements and progress in PE.

Working with and valuing LSAs

Research conducted by UNISON (2013) found that 95 per cent of head teachers believe that LSAs add value to schools and any attempt by government to reduce their number would have a negative impact on pupils with SEND and the smooth running of schools. This was a clear indicator of the value assigned to LSAs. Interestingly, LSAs in research by Maher and Vickerman (2018) did not feel nor experience this value. 'Poor pay' and excessive workloads were considered to be key indicators of the lack of value for the role of LSAs in schools. This was mentioned by both SENCOs and LSAs. LSAs also drew attention to the fact that they did not feel valued by some teachers either.

One way in which LSAs reported that they would feel more valued is if they were involved, even to a small degree, in the planning of lessons. Given that LSAs are specifically trained to facilitate inclusion, and that in many cases they work so closely with pupils that they best understand their needs and capabilities, this seems like a positive suggestion. It is important to acknowledge, as LSAs did in research conducted by Maher and Vickerman (2018), that involving LSAs in the planning of lessons will take more time from a teacher's already congested day. Therefore, we are suggesting that this collaboration is as time-efficient as possible. This can involve a quick conversation at opportune moments throughout the day to discuss specific pupils, activities and learning targets.

At the very least, it is important to appropriately brief LSAs before each lesson so that they know what is going to happen in the lesson and what is expected of them during the lesson. Too often, LSAs turn up to lessons without knowing what the lesson is about or what is expected of them, which can significantly hinder the extent to which they can facilitate the learning of the children they are expected to support (Maher and Vickerman 2018).

The training of LSAs

It is important to note that there is some research suggesting that some PE teachers consider the presence of LSAs as more of a hindrance than a help when it comes to the support provided by LSAs (e.g. Smith and Green 2004). This is largely because many LSAs are traditionally classroom-based, so do not have the knowledge, skills or experience to support inclusion in a more dynamic and physically-orientated subject such as PE. It has been said that much of the training LSAs experience is relevant to classroom-based subjects but, often, does not transfer easily to PE.

In this respect, LSAs in research conducted by Maher and Macbeth (2013) have called for more PE-specific continued professional development training within schools to prepare them for their role in PE. The limited training, it is important to note, is not necessarily because of a lack of available courses because training on inclusive PE and sport activities is currently provided by the English Federation of Disability Sport (EFDS), Youth Sport Trust (YST), Sports Coach UK (SCUK), and various national governing bodies (NGBs) and national disability sport organisations (NDSO). Instead, financial restrictions within and across schools, together with the prioritisation of English, Maths and Science as subject areas when it comes to LSA training, has meant that this call remains largely unanswered (Maher and Macbeth 2013).

Nonetheless, there is scope within schools for PE teachers and LSAs to work together to upskill each other. Teachers are subject experts and LSAs are inclusion experts. Therefore, each can learn from the other. This does not have to be particularly laborious or time-consuming. More, it could take the form of a brief conversation about content, pedagogy and inclusion before the planning of a lesson and again after the lesson. Here, we continue to promote the importance of reflective learning for PE teachers and LSAs.

Conclusion

Increasingly within education, you are likely to see multi-disciplinary partnership approaches to ensuring that children with SEND gain their full entitlement and accessibility to the PE curriculum. Consequently, it is vital that teachers have a thorough understanding of the range of services and support mechanism within and outside of the school that are on offer to help both children and teachers alike. What is critical in ensuring that these partnerships are effective is that each professional values and appreciates the individual role that each can offer to the child and each other in ensuring children with SEND receive the best support, care and education possible. In addition to the standard health and education therapists it may be appropriate for teachers to make contact with local disability sports clubs and national governing bodies in order to assist with children's development outside the formal school curriculum. Again, this is a critical element of not only supporting children with SEND as part of the curriculum, but also ensuring that they have access to agencies that can assist with their lifelong participation in physical activity outside of school. Consequently, teachers' commitment to holistic and multi-disciplinary partnership approaches is essential if children with SEND are to learn and progress in their PE lessons. It is hoped that in this chapter the discussion has gone some way to encouraging you to extend your understanding of other professional roles and how they can support children to have a positive PE experience.

Chapter 8

Opportunities outside the curriculum

Introduction and context

Although the focus of this book has largely been on core curriculum matters in inclusive PE, it is important to highlight how pupils with SEND can access activity outside the curriculum time through extra-curricular and/or community-based activities. This is important because children with SEND are just as entitled to sporting and extra-curricular physical activities as their age-peers. There are a number of organisations and initiatives aimed at providing activity for children alongside those specialist agencies who support children with SEND. Consequently, as part of their extended inclusive practice, PE teachers should seek to develop partnership links with such organisations. This is of particular relevance to Sport England's (2016) *Towards an Active Nation Strategy*, which encourages school–community links in order to ensure that the foundations of physical activity within the curriculum are built upon and extended after school into lifelong enjoyment and participation in sport.

In addition, with the Government's health agenda and concerns over increases in childhood obesity, the health of the nation's young children, including those with SEND, is a key area for action. Therefore, it has become increasingly important that children generally, and those with SEND in particular, engage in extra-curricular physical activities and other sporting opportunities outside of school in order to meet the DoH's (2011) guidelines, as discussed in Chapter 2. A lack of physical activity in childhood is linked intrinsically to obesity-related diseases in later life. However, through a combination of a healthy diet and regular physical activity from an early age, young people can radically reduce their chances of developing long-term illnesses such as diabetes and heart disease. A key component of fostering lifelong physical activity and healthy lifestyles is PE teachers, who have a duty to raise children's awareness of these issues and help children to create links with after school and community organisations to continue participation outside of the formal school curriculum.

Given the demise of the PESSCL and PESSYP strategies, a far greater onus has been placed on schools and PE teachers to encourage children and young people to engage in sport and physical activity outside of school. Satellite Clubs have been identified as one mechanism to link PE and school sport with sporting opportunities outside of school. By bringing existing sports clubs into educational settings, satellite clubs aim to 'create "bridges" between school and community sport and provide participants with opportunities to "transition" from Satellite Clubs to traditional community sports clubs' (Sport England 2017: 3). These are local sport and physical activity clubs that attempt to provide positive and enjoyable opportunities so that children and young people can become active and develop regular physical activity habits (Sport England 2017). Young people with disabilities are identified as an under-represented group in sport that should receive a targeted approach. In this respect, a report by Sport England (2017) suggests that these clubs have had a positive impact on the sports participation tendencies of young people with disabilities outside of school.

Task 8.1   Satellite Clubs

Reflect upon the Satellite Clubs described above in relation to your understanding of them and how you think they apply to children with SEND. Consider any potential issues or challenges you can see in facilitating the transition of children with SEND to these clubs. Also think about what you will need to do to address these issues and overcome the challenges.

The structure of disability sport

The structure of disability sport, like developments in PE for children with SEND, is evolving, and in 1997 Sport England's task force on the future of disability sport (Sport England 1997) recommended that disability sport be incorporated into the work of governing bodies of sport. There was a clear recognition, however, that this was not going to occur in the short term and that a considerable amount of work was going to have to be undertaken to achieve this objective. The EFDS was established in order to achieve the shift towards a more integrated approach to the provision of sport for children with SEND and adults with disabilities.

EFDS aims to expand sporting opportunities for people with disabilities and increase the numbers actively involved in sport. It also aims to ensure that people with disabilities are included in sporting opportunities, and to encourage a move towards more inclusive approaches of delivery. Its mission is to be the united voice of disability sport, seeking to promote inclusion and achieve equality of sporting opportunities for people with disabilities. As a result, EFDS intends to deliver this mission through a set of strategic aims:

- provide strategic leadership and direct support to get more disabled people participating in sport and physical activity;
- be recognised and respected as the authoritative voice for disabled people in sport and physical activity in England;

- be the central resource for research evidence relating to disabled people and sport;
- ensure that strong and effective engagement processes and partnerships are in place with National Governing Bodies (NGBs), County Sport Partnerships (CSPs), National Disability Sport Organisations (NDSOs);
- work collaboratively with disabled people and develop an effective platform for their engagement with sport and physical activity;
- ensure the provision of pathways to participation for disabled people in sport and physical activity through a dedicated events programme;
- influence and support the health and fitness industry to provide high quality inclusive services and provision;
- promote and develop specific programmes and activities to support the growth in participation of young disabled people within sport and physical activity;
- generate significant additional income and funding opportunities to support the participation of disabled people in sport and physical activity.

(EFDS 2017)

There are currently nine EFDS regions, where teachers can access information about local and national opportunities, each comprising membership of national disability sports organisations (NDSOs). The NDSOs are structured mostly around impairment-specific groups encompassing: British Blind Sport, Cerebral Palsy Sport, Dwarf Sports Association UK, LimbPower, Mencap, Special Olympics Great Britain, UK Deaf Sport and WheelPower. Whilst this method of categorisation arguably reinforces the medical model of disability, the organisations have long-established traditions, and the aim over time is to function through mainstream governing bodies of sport, and one umbrella disability governing body (EFDS). This will be in line with current thinking on evolving inclusive practice within both sport and PE. In addition, by agencies such as EFDS working alongside mainstream governing bodies of sport, and schools, it is envisaged that inclusive activity has real potential for success in the future. Consequently, it is crucial that PE teachers who support children with SEND have an in-depth appreciation of the extracurricular and out of school sporting agencies that can support and develop lifelong physical activity participation.

Classification of disability sport and the history of the Paralympic movement

According to Richter et al. (1992) classification systems have been widely used in sports to allow for fair and equitable starting points for competition. There is a distinction to be made, however, between definitions and rationales for 'medical' and 'functional' models of classification. Medical classifications are concerned with verifying minimum levels of disability, whilst a functional classification considers how an athlete performs in specific sports (Winnick and Poretta 2017). Consequently, it is through functional classification that the structure of disability sport for competition purposes is organised. The functional classification, as Richter et al. (1992) indicate, establishes a starting point for fair competition that takes account of how disability impacts upon performance in specific sports. The functional classification is characterised by over 40 separate physical profiles, and three categories for people with visual impairments. This system, although complex in relation to athletes with disabilities gaining classification (through assessment by a medical practitioner), has worked well in relation to competition for individuals with a physical disability (Depauw and Gavron 2005).

The situation is more complex, and less clear, when it comes to judgements on how 'intellectual cognition' relates to performance in sport, and this has been a subject of much debate at international level, at events such as the Paralympic Games. The Paralympic Games (parallel games) are the equivalent of the Olympic Games, but are mainly concerned with provision for athletes with physical disabilities and those with visual impairments. People with hearing impairments compete in the World Deaf Games, whilst people with learning disabilities have the Special Olympics and a separate Paralympic movement. This categorised and distinctive organisational approach has served disability sport well over the years. However, in light of more recent moves to inclusive environments there is significant debate on how this should be reflected in relation to competition for disabled groups and individuals. Consequently, whilst in school sport and PE the shift is currently towards inclusive activity, there will always be a place for disability sports activity through which children with SEND can compete on relatively even playing fields. As a result, teachers will need to have a full appreciation of the structures of disability sport and the nature of classification systems if they are to enable children with SEND to access these structures.

Task 8.2   Researching disability sport organisations

Take time to undertake some research into organisations such as the English Federation for Disability Sport and the British Paralympic Association. You may even wish to talk to your local sport development officer to gain a more localised picture of the specific arrangements for disability sport. Once you have done this, reflect upon how these agencies can help you become an effective teacher in making links between the formal school PE curriculum and lifelong physical activity.

The development of the Paralympic movement and disability sport is well documented (Roth et al. 2017; Winnick and Porretta 2017), with international competition in disability sport starting in 1948 at Stoke Mandeville as part of the 14th Olympic Games held in London. The background to the development of the Stoke Mandeville games was to include sport as part of a rehabilitation process for people with spinal cord injuries. This was within the context of innovatory practice, which acknowledged that people with disabilities could still participate and compete in sport (and at high levels) despite any limiting mobility factors. The first Paralympics were held in Rome in 1960 and have developed and increased in size significantly, culminating in the largest games in London in 2012.

However, it was in Sydney that for the first time some disability events were held as part of the mainstream Olympic Games, whilst the separate Paralympics had regular crowd attendances of 90,000 spectators. This demonstrated the interest and recognition of how far disability sport had come in recent years and reinforces the shift towards more inclusive approaches to sport and PE. In addition, there are many lessons to be learned from countries such as Australia in fostering and developing the passion and interest in both physical participation and spectator sport, which resulted in the largest attendances at for London 2012 at any Paralympic games to date.

London 2012 was of further interest in that it had the explicit aim of changing societal attitudes towards disability and using sport as vehicle for creating a better world for people with disabilities (Hodges et al. 2014). The extent to which these ambitious targets have been achieved has been subject to much debate. A report by Hodges et al. (2014: 4) does suggest that there had been a 'reduction in discomfort when watching disabled people on screen' and 'greater confidence and less anxiety in talking about disability sports'. There was also reported shifts from only seeing the disability to focusing more on the sporting excellence of the Paralympic athletes.

The longer-term impact of the Paralympic Games on societal attitudes to people with disabilities is yet to be seen. The same can also be said of Rio 2016 as we wait for the dust to settle. The build up to Rio 2016 was problematic to say the least. Against a backdrop of a struggling Brazilian economy and some social and political unrest, only 12 per cent of Paralympic tickets had been purchased three weeks before the first event and there was a delay in sending travel grants of $8 million to poorer countries. To avert the lowest attendances in Paralympic history, money was borrowed and ticket prices slashed, resulting in the second highest attended Paralympic Games in its history.

Finding local opportunities and creating school–community links

There are two key pathways that can be followed in the development of school–community links for children with SEND as part of an extension to the formal PE curriculum – disability-specific sports clubs, or mainstream sports clubs (Vickerman and Hayes 2013). As part of Sport England's strategies for sport over a long period of time, most local authorities have established sports development officers who know where local sports clubs meet, and how accessible they are to people with disabilities. Some local authorities produce directories of sports clubs that provide opportunities for people with disabilities, and sports development officers can act as invaluable links between school PE departments and local sports communities.

Governing bodies of sport are taking a more inclusive approach to their delivery. For instance, the Amateur Swimming Association have teamed up with British Disability Swimming to develop a resource to help swimming teachers, coaches, schools, and parents with identifying and teaching swimmers with disabilities. EFDS's Ability Counts programme has worked with the Football Association to ensure that professional clubs include young people with disabilities in their community programmes, and local sports disability groups provide a good way of bridging the link between school and the community. Development work in disability sport is mainly concentrating on providing people with disabilities with more choice on the range of activities that they can become involved in, within inclusive, adapted, and disability sport settings.

Clearly, there is still a considerable way to go before total inclusion and mainstreaming of disability sport is fully realised. It is easy to be critical, but it should be recognised that inclusion is becoming a reality (Depauw and Doll-Tepper 2000) and not just a possibility, and strategies such as those by Sport England, and the development of EFDS, are complementing similar work being undertaken within the PE curriculum. Initiatives such as the Youth Sport Trust's TOP Sportsability programmes have also added a new dimension to the area of inclusive PE provision. The resources provided by the Youth Sport Trust has been aimed specifically at special schools and mainstream schools with pupils with SEND.

TOP Sportsability is a free online resource for schools that offers practical advice to teachers, learning support staff, and other sports practitioners. It consists of video clips and downloadable content showing ideas and strategies around the inclusion of young people with disabilities. It is divided into three sections:

- **user manual** – shows how to use the resource and establishes basic principles and models of inclusion;
- **disability sport and adapted games** – features the sports in the original TOP Sportsability plus some new activities;
- **sports adaptations** – consists of traditional 'mainstream' sports adapted for the widest possible range of abilities.

Whilst this equipment is aimed at young people with SEND, all young people can join in playing by the same rules as their peers with disabilities. In addition, five separate games were identified by Youth Sport Trust to be used to help those pupils with severe disabilities. These games are known as boccia (a bowls-type game), table cricket, table hockey, polybat (an adapted version of table tennis), and goalball (a game played by visually impaired people). Four of these games have pathways for young people to go on and progress from recreational level through to national, international and Paralympic competition, which further supports the need to provide clear, consistent and achievable pathways for children with SEND to progress through in PE, school sport, and wider community sporting opportunities.

The tabletop games, although designed primarily to be played on a table tennis table, are versatile enough to be played at most tables. Polybat was designed for children with SEND who have control and co-ordination difficulties. The development of a glove bat has ensured that pupils who find it hard to grip a bat can handle the polybat, and therefore can still participate successfully. In addition, activities such as goal ball (a three-a-side game developed for visually impaired people) can involve sighted players in which everyone wears adapted goggles. This is an example of 'reverse inclusion' (Roth et al. 2017; Winnick and Porretta 2017), where sighted people can be included in a disability-specific game as part of a PE teacher's use of the 'inclusion spectrum' noted earlier.

Task 8.3   The findings from the Sport England Survey

Using the table below, reflect upon the issues relating to the physical activity participation tendencies of children with disabilities. You should try to identify what and why the issues exist, then consider how you could address these issues as part of your own practice.

Key issues	What issues exist, and why?	What strategies can you employ to address these issues and concerns?
Young people with disabilities participate less frequently than their age-peers in curriculum PE		
Young people with disabilities participate less frequently in sport and physical activity during lunch-time than their age-peers		
Young people with disabilities participate in a narrower range of sports and physical activities than their age peers both inside and outside of school		
Young people with disabilities participate less frequently than their age-peers in sport and physical activity outside of school		

Whilst more opportunities are being created for young people with disabilitiesto participate either recreationally or competitively in sport, for schools and their PE teachers it is important to know where and how to access the network of provision available at both local and/or national level. This situation could be improved through better-informed partnerships between school PE departments and disability organisations, both nationally and regionally, and should be seen as a developing role within a PE department's inclusive structures (Vickerman and Hayes 2013).

Conclusion

It is important that all young people, whether they have SEND or not, have the opportunities to participate, develop and excel in PE, school sport and community based lifelong physical activity. This is important for their social, mental and physical health and well-being. However, in order to ensure that children with SEND receive meaningful opportunities, it is essential that teachers take a dual approach, first by recognising specialist disability sports organisations, and second by encouraging mainstream organisations to support children as well. A central part of the success or otherwise, however, is the teacher of PE having a full grasp of some of the potential issues and barriers noted in this chapter and an appreciation of the local and national agencies that are available both for advice and support to pupils, parents, the school, and you as the teacher.

Chapter 9

Hearing the voices of children with special educational needs and disabilities

Introduction

Teachers and academics within the field of PE are recognising the importance of understanding the views and experiences of children with SEND (Farr 2018; Wilhelmsen and Sørensen 2017). Including children in research as active participants is also assisting in uncovering their lived experiences, and is helping teachers to appreciate the needs of children with SEND. These ultimately then enable teachers to plan, and deliver inclusive lessons (Tant and Watelain 2016). Consequently, the 'lived' experiences of pupils with SEND in PE are critical to gaining full insight from all stakeholders' perspectives. Indeed, if this were absent, a critical aspect of understanding the practice of inclusive education would be lost. Therefore, this chapter aims to, first, provide a rationale for seeking the views and experiences of children with SEND and discuss how researchers and teachers can elicit information from these children. Next, the chapter will explore pupil views and experiences of PE to ensure that activities are more inclusive, before finally provide a framework for ensuring those who support children with SEND in PE are cognisant of the diverse factors integral to a positive learning experience.

Why is it important to hear children with SEND's voices?

According to Wang (2016), learning is enhanced when young people engage in the decisions and experiences that impact upon them. Teachers should therefore listen to the views of children with SEND in order to develop provision that meets their specific needs (Sonday and Gretschel 2016). This can also aid children's motivation, engagement, self-esteem, and ensure they feel valued. The United Nations (UN) Convention of the Rights of the Child (UN 1992) reinforces this view by stating children have the right to be consulted about matters affecting their lives. Indeed, since the Convention was introduced, children have much more openly been recognised as key stakeholders in decisions and activities relating to their own lives. Children with SEND having the opportunity to have a voice goes a long way towards developing their personal skills, and recognising their voice (and views) as important. Moreover, research by Hutzler et al. (2002) and Woolfson (2007) demonstrates that children with SEND benefit from active consultation. Furthermore, children with SEND can provide important information about how well they consider they are being included in education (Vickerman and Coates 2009).

Whilst this particular chapter focuses on hearing the voices of children with SEND in PE (Fitzgerald 2005, 2007; Maher 2017), there are many more studies outside this specific National Curriculum subject area. However, whether you focus on PE (Mihajlovic 2017), or broader areas of children with SEND's life (Jones 2005), the definitions and interpretations of consultation and empowerment remain common. Whilst no single definition of pupil voice and consultation describes the process fully, there are key words commonly referenced. Words such as 'empowerment', 'participation', 'engagement', 'consultation', 'facilitation', and 'giving voice' are regularly used in literature to describe the process and strategies for including children with SEND in decisions that impact them (Wang 2016; Wilhelmsen and Sørensen 2017).

Task 9.1   Hearing the voices of children with SEND

Using the table below, review the words noted above describing commonly referenced terms around pupil voice, and write down what you understand by their meaning. Then, think of a practical example in the context of PE in which you may use that word to work alongside children with SEND. You may wish to undertake this task alone, and then discuss it with someone to clarify your understanding. Two boxes are completed as examples to assist you.

Term	Definition	Example within the context of PE with children with SEND
Empowerment		
Participation		Allowing two bounces of a tennis ball on one side of the court so that a child with SEND has more opportunity for success.
Engagement	A process of actively listening, discussing, and working to address individual needs.	
Consultation		
Facilitation		
Giving voice		

Consultation and empowerment of children with SEND is not a new concept; it dates back as far as the revised SEN *Code of Practice* (DfES 2001b). This Code introduced the notion of pupil participation, advocating that children with SEND have a right to express an opinion and to have that fully considered. What this does for you when working with children with SEND is place a responsibility on you to make 'every reasonable endeavour' to obtain their views, and where necessary utilise a range of communication and engagement strategies to facilitate this (Sato and Haegele 2017).

The revised *Code of Practice: 0–25 years* (DfE/DOH 2015), and the Ofsted Inspection Framework (OFSTED 2017), both acknowledge the importance of involving pupils, including those with SEND, to advocate their views and experiences of schooling. Furthermore, research demonstrates that the regular involvement of children with SEND in the decisions and educational experiences concerned with them, often results in tangible positive impacts upon educational outcomes (Lambe 2011).

Including pupils in the development of their education is founded upon sound research (Tant and Watelain 2016; Wang 2016). Indeed, concepts of 'assessment for learning' (Earl 2012) promote the positive impact of children with SEND sharing learning objectives, setting goals, targets, and sharing feedback. Furthermore, research by Chappuis (2015), and Coates and Vickerman (2010) suggests that children with SEND are more likely to take ownership of their learning and strive towards their targets if they have positively engaged in the initial process.

Children with SEND have a diverse range of conditions and individual needs. At times, it may be a challenge to engage fully with them, particularly when they have extensive communication and/or social interaction needs. However, whilst some children with SEND may have significant communication difficulties, it is still important to give them the opportunity to advocate their needs (Maher 2016). Here, it is vital to provide information that is meaningful and accessible. This may require the use of teaching assistants, parents, carers, and/or speech and language therapists to aid interaction and engagement.

To ensure children with SEND's participation is inclusive, the social model of disability provides a framework for inclusive participation. The social model seeks to change attitudes and minimise the barriers (Wang 2016) preventing children with SEND being afforded the same opportunities as their peers. Moreover, the social model describes disability as created from interactions between someone with an impairment, and the barriers that exist in the environment. Barriers could include physical, social, emotional, policies, and practices. Thus, a key mechanism to address potential barriers for children with SEND in PE is to adopt the social model and recognise a lack of accessibility may be due to factors such as inflexible teaching, learning, and assessment strategies (Hodge, Lieberman and Murata 2017). Consulting the child, who often is the expert when it comes to their disability and particular needs (and may have experienced particular scenarios before), may aid better inclusion and minimise barriers to participation. This approach contrasts with medical models of disability where a child with SEND is considered the barrier and they must adapt to fit into existing PE lessons and wider school structures (Lambe 2011).

Strategies for consulting children with SEND

Based on the discussion above, there are a range of approaches you could adopt to ensure children with SEND are engaged in decisions about their schooling and life choices. Examples of approaches you could consider include:

- ensuring pupils with SEND are involved in any annual reviews of progress;
- embed choice and empowerment as an integral element of your teaching and learning with children with SEND. This could include visual clues, objects of reference, pictures and symbols to aid decision-making;
- involve teaching assistants, parents, professionals who know the child well. Individuals who know the child with SEND well may be able to recognise particular body language, eye gaze and/or patterns of communication to further assist you;
- talk to the child with SEND, and those who know them best to appreciate how they convey their needs;
- introduce cards with colours or images for children for children with SEND so they can learn to point to what they like, or do not like;
- identify pictures that a child with SEND can understand to identify their emotions, and/or rank their views, opinions and choices.

Task 9.2   The 'Eight P' inclusive PE framework for including children with SEND

Based on the examples above, reflect on your own style and approaches to including children with SEND in PE. It is important when thinking about this task, to ensure you have an open mind, high expectations of all children, and a readiness to adapt your practice (Medcalf 2008). Whilst it is important to think flexibly and openly about the diversity of methods by which you can include children with SEND, there is

(continued)

(continued)

ways the danger that too much flexibility can leave you with a feeling of being lost and with no context or concepts to attach your thoughts. As a result, the 'Eight P' framework (Coates and Vickerman 2009) encourages you to work through a series of key aspects of inclusive PE provision for children with SEND. In reading the 'Eight P Framework' below, use this to clarify your understanding of inclusive education, whilst also identifying examples of how to engage children with SEND in decision that affect them.

The 'Eight P' inclusive PE framework for including children with SEN in PE

	Description and interpretation	Give an example of what this means to giving children with SEND a voice in PE
Philosophy	Check your understanding of what the principles, concepts and contexts of inclusion stand for and their relationship to children with SEND in PE. Try to be clear about what your philosophical standpoint is on inclusive education.	
Purposeful	Write a list of the rationales behind strategies for including children with SEND in PE. List how entitlement and accessibility can be created.	
Proactive	Are you ready to identify challenges and solutions to issues and problems you may face when including children with SEND in PE? How do you ensure you adopt flexible approaches and maintain a personal desire to be innovative and creative with your practice?	
Partnership	Inclusion needs to take place within a context of consultation and negotiation as part of a holistic approach to PE for children with SEND. List who you may speak to for advice.	
Process	Recognise that inclusion takes time and you may not get it right the first time. However, being prepared to try out new strategies and learn from the experience of diversity of styles and experiences will aid your learning.	
Policy	Institutional policies on equality of opportunity and inclusion in PE will demonstrate commitment to and support for the principles of entitlement and accessibility. The key, however, to any policy on inclusion is the impact it has in making a difference, whether that is strategically or at a practical level. How can you ensure policies are effective?	

Pedagogy	*Recognise that in any inclusive process, the key aspect of most significance is the teaching, learning, and assessment activity that takes place with the teacher and child with SEND. As part of this process, teachers need to adopt flexible approaches, have high expectations and be prepared to modify and adapt as part of their pedagogical practice.*
Practice	*If you take note, and discuss, reflect and debate on all the points above it offers the best chance of you making a difference to the child with SEND in working towards ensuring they gain successful PE experiences.*

Understanding the 'Eight P Framework' and its relationship to pupil voice

The 'Eight P Framework' can be used to examine a range of aspects of inclusive education. For the purpose of this chapter, it will be considered within the context of giving children with SEND in PE a voice. The first feature to consider is a need to recognise the **philosophy** behind inclusion, and its relationships to basic and fundamental human rights. This requires consideration of how human rights are supported as a society through statutory and non-statutory guidance such as the SEND *Code of Practice* (DfE/DOH 2015). Pragmatically, it requires you to spend time engaging in understanding philosophical theories and principles, identified in earlier chapters of this book. Moreover, you should consider what they mean in relation to empowering children with SEND to advocate their views and experiences.

In order to reflect on your own philosophical standpoint to inclusive PE, you must embrace a **purposeful** approach to fulfilling the requirements of children with SEND. Time should be spent actively examining your own philosophical standpoints in order to gain a clear appreciation of the rationale and arguments behind inclusive education. Thus, as practitioners or policy makers, we must be ready to ask questions about past, present, and future practices, and the relevance of them to the successful inclusion of children with SEND in PE. Indeed, being prepared to reflect and learn from your own, and others (including children with SEND) experiences through open dialogue, should enable you to gain a greater insight into why hearing the voices of children is an essential aspect of delivering high quality PE.

In order to achieve high quality PE for children with SEND, you must be **proactive** in the development, implementation, and review of inclusive PE, and consult actively with a range of stakeholders. This will ensure the views and opinions of all stakeholders are considered in order to create co-ordinated and coherent provision through **partnership** and collaborative approaches. Indeed, it is vital that we see the process of including children with SEND in PE as a holistic partnership, and we do not see ourselves as isolated figures in striving to meet the needs of particular individuals.

Inclusive PE for children with SEND requires a recognition and commitment to modify, adapt, and change existing teaching, learning, and assessment strategies, policies and practices in order to facilitate full access and entitlement to the curriculum. The development of inclusive PE must be recognised as part of a **process** that evolves, emerges, and changes over time. Any process involves dynamic discussion and debate, and a desire to learn from mistakes as well as celebrate successes.

In summary, the 'Eight P Framework' sets out to ensure inclusion is reflected within **policy** documentation, as a means of monitoring, reviewing and evaluating delivery. This openly articulates publicly how agencies are going to respond to inclusive practice, and when necessary be used as a means of holding people to account. However, we must all ultimately recognise the need to move policies through into the **pedagogical** practices to ensure you have the necessary skills to deliver inclusive PE to children with SEND. Consequently, whilst philosophies and processes are vital, they must in due course be measured in terms of effective and successful inclusive **practice** that values person-centred approaches to the education of children with SEND.

How can you measure successful consultation?

Successful inclusion, according to Connors and Stalker (2007) and Flecha (2014), requires decision-makers and individuals with SEND to have informed choice with regard to the nature of their involvement in physical activity. In order to facilitate choice, there is a need for agencies and individuals to work within a culture that offers a commitment to improve the expertise of teachers, and offer flexible learning and instructional environments to meet the individual needs of children with SEND (Lambe and Bones 2006; Fakolade et al. 2017).

Hodge et al. (2017) suggest, for example, there is a great need to examine concepts of empowerment and what they actually mean in practice for a child with SEND in PE. Cohen et al. (2014) support this view, linking the concepts of inclusion and empowerment, based on the belief that personal empowerment of children with SEND is an integral component in helping to understand the inclusion process. Indeed, they found over half of the negative physical activity experiences of children with SEND attributed failure as due to a lack of empowerment. As a result, children with SEND advocated the use of consultation as a means of addressing this issue in the future, and authors such Coates and Vickerman (2016), and Georgeson et al. (2014), suggest consultation and empowerment of children with SEND are important mechanisms in understanding the issues that matter to children.

The establishment of mechanisms for consultation and empowerment are vital ingredients in gaining a full appreciation of all the perspectives of inclusive PE for children with SEND. Goodwin and Watkinson (2000) undertook a study titled 'good days and bad days' were they examined children with SEND's experiences of inclusive PE. Although this study took place nearly 20 years ago, the issues they identified are still pertinent in ensuring we listen to the voices of children with SEND. Goodwin and Watkinson (2000) noted children with SEND described good days in PE as being focused around having a sense of belonging, skilful participation and sharing in the benefits of engagement and participation in the lesson. In contrast, bad days were described as being focused around social isolation, competence being questioned and restricted participation. If we are genuinely to 'hear the voices of the children' then we must take note of these reflections by the pupils we support (Coates and Vickerman 2009).

Concluding thoughts – children's different experiences

Use the table below to review what and why you think children have different PE experiences, and the range of strategies you could employ to address any points of concern whilst celebrating aspects of success.

This chapter has offered opportunities to focus on strategies to empower children with SEND to speak up and advocate their needs. Consulting children with SEND has grown rapidly over recent years (Fitzgerald 2005, 2007) and in the majority of cases these experiences have been positive for children and teachers alike. You should be prepared to seize opportunities

Good days/bad days	What and why is the experience occurring?	What strategies can we employ to celebrate success, whilst identifying solutions to problems?
Good days Experiencing a sense of belonging		
Good days Engaging in skillful participation		
Good days Sharing in the benefits of engagement and participation		
Bad days Focused around social isolation		
Bad days Competence being questioned		
Bad days Focused upon restricted participation and engagement		

and problems, and challenge your practice (MacConville 2007), alongside committing to adopt flexible teaching, learning and assessment approaches.

As the Joseph Rowntree Foundation (2001) notes, 'consulting with children and young people has also been promoted in good practice guides across a range of government initiatives, including Early Years Child Care and Development Partnerships'. Moreover, designing services around the needs of children by asking them their views and opinions is a critical component in ensuring provision meets everyone's needs. In closing, read the quotes from the Joseph Rowntree Foundation (2001) consultative group of disabled children. The quotes are powerful reminders of why hearing the voices of children with SEND are so important to ensuring inclusive PE is a positive experience for all.

'Don't blame us or have a go at us'
'We do have feelings'
'We're just like other children'
'Show respect, and don't patronise us'
'Take your time and make sure you understand'
'Talk directly to us, not just our parents, or our carers'
'Don't be scared to ask questions'
'Really listen and understand'
'Make sure you really understand us because I have seen carers, parents and other people who didn't even know or can't be bothered to find out how we say yes or no'.
'Don't be scared'
'Learn from young people'
'Show an interest in us, make it more than just a job'

(Joseph Rowntree Foundation 2001)

Further reading

The context for inclusion

Association for Physical Education (AfPE) website: www.afpe.org.uk
This website offers useful links to PE documentation and information on teaching and supporting children with SEND, including practical strategies, safe practice and resource guides.

English Federation for Disability Sport (EFDS) website: www.efds.net
This website offers a range of links to local, regional, national and international agencies involved in the promotion and development of disability sport. The website has many useful links and a dedicated research section, which updates you on current initiatives and practices.

Peer, L. and Reid, G. (2016), *Special Educational Needs: A Guide for Inclusive Practice* **(2nd edition), Sage, London** The edited collection provides a broad and systemic overview of SEND in education, ranging from inclusive policy, provision and practice; perspectives from practitioners, barriers to inclusion, and the importance of working in partnership.

Children with Special Educational Needs and Disabilities

Oliver, M. (2013), 'The Social Model of Disability: Thirty Years On', *Disability and Society*, **28(7), 1024–1026** In this short paper Mike Oliver, the person credited with developing the social model of disability, restates his view of what the social model was and what he sees as its potential for improving the lives of people with disabilities.

Reindal, S. (2008), A Social Relational Model of Disability: A Theoretical Framework for Special Needs Education?, *European Journal of Special Needs Education*, **23(2), 135–146** This paper analyses critically both the medical and social models of disability in order to develop a basis for arguing for the social-relational model of disability.

Contact a Family (CAF Directory) www.cafamily.org.uk Contact a Family is the only UK-wide charity providing advice, information, and support to the parents of children with disabilities. It states that, across the UK, a child is diagnosed with a severe disability every 25 minutes and over 98 per cent of children with disabilities are cared for at home by a parent or other family member. This directory puts parents and those who support disabled children in touch with each other to offer mutual support and insight into children's specific needs.

Movement, learning and ranges of special educational need

Donnelly, F., Mueller, S., and Gallahue, D. (2016), *Developmental Physical Education for All Children: Theory into Practice*, Human Kinetics, Champaign, IL This book provides an interesting and useful insight into the movement concepts and frameworks, as well as motor development and learning among all children.

Place, K. and Hodge, S. (2001), 'Social Inclusion of Students with Physical Disabilities in General Physical Education: A Behavioural Analysis', *Adapted Physical Activity Quarterly*, 18, 389–404 This research paper offers a useful insight into the inclusion of children with physical disabilities in PE. The paper offers a range of research and theoretical applications to support the study's findings. Any teacher who is involved in planning, delivering, and evaluating inclusive PE should read this research paper as a starting point for understanding many of the issues and challenges that may occur.

Winnick, J. and Porretta, D. (2017), *Adapted Physical Education and Sport* (6th edition), Human Kinetics, Leeds This book provides a detailed overview of a wide range of disabilities and their associated characteristics. The book also gives a detailed account of teaching and learning strategies and begins to interpret what adapted PE actually consists of and what methods need to be employed to ensure the needs of children with SEND are met.

The Physical Education National Curriculum and inclusion

Auxter, D., Pyfer, J., and Hueltig, C. (2009), *Principles and Methods of Adapted Physical Education and Recreation* (11th edition), McGraw-Hill, New York This book offers an insight into several key principles for adapting and modifying PE lessons. The book is a useful starting point to extend your reading on the methods and strategies you may wish to consider as part of the development of your teaching and learning activity with children with SEND.

Hutzler, Y., Fliess, O., Chacham, A. and Auweele, Y. (2002), 'Perspectives of Children with Physical Disabilities on Inclusion and Empowerment: Supporting and Limiting Factors', *Adapted Physical Activity Quarterly*, 19, 300–317 This research article offers an overview of the potential barriers to including children with SEND in physical activities. The article will help you to reflect upon some of the issues that can often be problematic with inclusive activity and will help you to take steps in advance to address these.

Vickerman, P. and Hayes, S. (2013), 'Special Educational Needs and Disability in Physical Education', in Stidder, G. and Hayes, S. (eds), *Equity and Inclusion in Physical Education*, Routledge, London This book chapter offers a range of strategies for including children with SEN in PE.

Planning for and assessing children with special educational needs and disabilities

AfPE (Association for Physical Education) (2014), *Guidance of Assessment: National Curriculum (2014)*, AfPE, Worcester, UK This resource has been created to help teachers to develop effective assessment strategies to engage, support, and motivate pupils to become competent, confident, creative and reflective movers.

Hay, P. and Penney, D. (2013), *Assessment in Physical Education: A Sociocultural Perspective*, Routledge, London This book analyses critically assessment in PE by focusing on developing assessment 'messages', enacting assessment and promoting assessment literacy.

Lopez-Pastor, V., Kirk, D., Lorente-Catalan, E., MacPhail, A., and Macdonald, D. (2013), 'Alternative Assessment in Physical Education: A Review of International Literature', *Sport, Education and Society*, 18(1), 57–76 This paper provides an overview of the international literature on assessment in school physical education. An account of both traditional and alternative forms of assessment is offered.

Teaching and learning strategies

Rink, J. (2014), *Teaching Physical Education for Learning* (7th edition), McGraw-Hill, Boston, MA This user-friendly text emphasises teaching strategies and theories to give future teachers a foundation for designing effective learning experiences.

Mosston, M. and Ashworth, S. (2001), *Teaching Physical Education* (5th edition), Macmillan, London This book offers teachers a foundation for understanding the decision-making structures that exist in all teaching/learning environments and for recognising the variables that increase effectiveness while teaching physical education

Norwich, B. (2002), 'Education, Inclusion and Individual Differences: Recognising and Resolving Dilemmas', *British Journal of Education Studies*, 50(4), 482–502 This journal article offers an insight into the challenges that are posed in offering person-centred and individualised approaches to education. It looks at the tension between taking whole group approaches in contrast to individualised learning and is a useful prompt for further reflection and debate.

Multi-disciplinary approaches and working in partnership

Hallett, F. and Hallett, G. (2010), *Transforming the Role of the SENCO: Achieving the National Award for SEN Coordination*, McGraw-Hill, Maidenhead This book analyses and critiques the characteristics and practice of the SENCO role at an academic level suitable to the new National Award.

Maher, A. (2017), '"We've Got a Few Who Don't Go to PE" Learning Support Assistant and Special Educational Needs Coordinator Views on Inclusion in Physical Education in England', *European Physical Education Review*, 23(2), 257–270 This paper analyses issues relating to the inclusion of children with SEND in PE from the perspectives of SENCOs and LSAs.

Vickerman, P. and Blundell, M. (2012), 'English Learning Support Assistants' Experiences of Including Children with Special Educational Needs in Physical Education', *European Journal of Special Needs Education*, 27(2), 143–156 This study examined the views, opinions and experiences of LSAs within England in relation to their perceived competence and confidence in supporting children with SEND in PE.

Opportunities outside the curriculum

Youth Sport Trust: www.youthsporttrust.org The Youth Sport Trust is a charity established in 1994 to effect change and to build a brighter future for young people in sport. Integral to its core purposes is the inclusion of children with disabilities, and they have established a series of resources cards and equipment bags to address this specific area.

Haycock, D. and Smith, A. (2011), 'Still "More of the Same for the More-Able?" Including Young Disabled People and Pupils with

Special Educational Needs in Extra-Curricular Physical Education', *Sport, Education and Society*, 16(4), 507–526 This paper examines the extent and ways in which PE teachers have endeavoured to incorporate pupils with SEND in extra-curricular PE.

Sport England (2017), 'Evaluation of Satellite Clubs: Final Report' [online] Available at: www.sportengland.org/media/11778/sport-england-evaluation-of-satellite-clubs-final-report-executive-summary-june-2017.pdf This report evaluates the impact of satellite clubs in relation to bridging the gap between school and community sport.

Hearing the voices of children with Special Educational Needs and Disabilities

Coates, J. and Vickerman, P. (2010), 'Empowering Children with Special Educational Needs to Speak Up: Experiences of Inclusive Physical Education', *Disability and Rehabilitation*, 32(18), 1517–1526 This article examines the views of children with SEND in relation to their inclusion and experiences of physical education. It embraces the perspectives of children in mainstream and special schools as a means of understanding the similarities and differences between the two different types of provision.

Goodwin, L. and Watkinson, J. (2000), 'Inclusive Physical Education from the Perspectives of Students with Physical Disabilities', *Adapted Physical Activity Quarterly*, 17, 144–160 This research paper picks up on and develops the concepts of good and bad days for children with SEN in PE. The article is worth reading as it is one of the few papers in circulation that has looked at the consultation of children and their views on the inclusion process.

Jackson, L. (2002), *Freaks, Geeks and Asperger Syndrome: A User Guide to Adolescence*, Jessica Kingsley Publishers, London This book offers a fascinating insight into the life and experiences of a young adolescent boy with Asperger's syndrome. Luke Jackson's personal reflections on his school experiences offer a real insight into his hopes, fears and points of celebration. It is a must-read for any teacher wishing to look at aspects of consultation and empowerment.

Bibliography

AfPE (Association for Physical Education) (2014), *Guidance of Assessment: National Curriculum* (2014), AfPE, Worcester, UK.

Ainscow, M. (1994), *Special Needs in the Classroom: A Teacher Education Guide*, Jessica Kingsley Publishers/UNESCO Publishing, London.

Ainscow, M. (1999), *Understanding the Development of Inclusive Schools*, Falmer Press, London.

Ainscow, M., Farrell, D., Tweddle, D., and Malkin, G. (1999), *Effective Practice in Inclusion and in Special and Mainstream Schools Working Together*, HMSO, London.

Alborz, A., Pearson, D., Farrell, P., and Howes, A. (2009), *The Impact of Adult Support Staff on Pupils and Mainstream Schools: A Systematic Review of Evidence*, EPPI-Centre, Social Science Research Unit, Institute of Education, University of London, London.W

Armstrong, F., Armstrong, D., and Barton, L. (eds) (2016), *Inclusive Education: Policy, Contexts, and Comparative Perspectives*, Routledge, London.

Artiles, A. (1998), 'The Dilemma of Difference: Enriching the Disproportionality Discourse with Theory and Context', *Journal of Special Education*, 32(1), 32–36.

Atkinson, H. and Black, K. (2006), *The Experiences of Young Disabled People Participating in PE, School Sport and Extra-Curricular Activities in Leicestershire and Rutland*, Institute of Youth Sport/Peter Harrison Centre for Disability Sport, Loughborough University, Loughborough.

Avramadis, E. and Norwich, B. (2002), 'Teachers' Attitudes Towards Integration/ Inclusion: A Review of the Literature', *European Journal of Special Needs Education*, 17(2), 129–147.

Bailey, R. (1999), 'Physical Education: Action, Play, Movement', in Riley, J. and Prentice, R. (eds), *The Primary Curriculum 7–11*, Chapman, London.

Bailey, R. (2001), *Teaching Physical Education: A Handbook for Primary and Secondary Teachers*, Kogan Page, London.

Ballard, K. (1997), 'Researching Disability and Inclusive Education: Participation, Construction and Interpretation', *International Journal of Inclusive Education*, 1(3), 243–256.

Barton, L. (1997), 'Inclusive Education: Romantic, Subversive or Realistic?' *International Journal of Inclusive Education*, 1(30), 231–242.

Barton, L. (ed.) (1998), *The Politics of Special Educational Needs*, Falmer Press, London.

Bassett, D., Haldenby, A., Tanner, W., and Trewhitt, K. (2010), *Every Teacher Matters*, Reform, London.

Block, M. and Volger, E. (1994), 'Inclusion in Regular Physical Education: The Research Base', *Journal of Physical Education, Recreation and Dance*, 65(1), 40–44.

Booth, T., Ainscow, M., Black-Hawkins, K., Vaughan, M., and Shaw, L. (2000), *Index for Inclusion: Developing Learning and Participation in Schools*, Centre for Studies on Inclusive Education, Bristol.

Boyd, B., Odom, S., Humphreys, B., and Sam, A. (2010), 'Infants and Toddlers with Autism Spectrum Disorder: Early Identification and Early Intervention', *Journal of Early Intervention*, 32(2), 75–98.

Bruner, J. (1971), *The Relevance of Education*, Norton, New York.

Brown, J. and Doveston, M. (2014), 'Short Sprint or an Endurance Test: The Perceived Impact of the National Award for Special Educational Needs Coordination', *Teacher Development*, 18(4), 495–510.

Carroll, H. (1972), 'The Remedial Teaching of Reading: An Evaluation', *Remedial Education*, 7(1), 10–15.

Carroll, B. (1994), *Assessment in Physical Education. A Teacher's Guide to the Issues*, Falmer, London.

Central Advisory Council for Education (1967) *Children and their Primary Schools*, HMSO, London.

Chappuis, J. (2015), *Seven Strategies of Assessment for Learning*, Pearson, New Jersey.

Clark, C., Dyson, A., and Millward, A. (1995a), 'Towards Inclusive Schools: Mapping the Field', in Clark, C., Dyson, A., and Millward, A. (eds), *Towards Inclusive Schools*, David Fulton, London.

Clark, C., Dyson, A., Millward, A., and Skidmore, D. (1995b), 'Dialectical Analysis, Special Needs and Schools as Organisations', in Clark, C., Dyson, A., and Millward, A. (eds), *Towards Inclusive Schools*, David Fulton, London.

Clark, C., Dyson, A., Millward, A., and Skidmore, D. (1997), *New Directions in Special Needs: Innovations in Mainstream Schools*, Cassell, London.

Coates, J. and Vickerman, P. (2009), 'Let the Children have their Say: Children with Special Educational Needs and their Experiences of Physical Education – A Review', *Support for Learning*, 23(4), 168–175.

Coates, J. and Vickerman P. (2010), 'Empowering Children with Special Educational Needs to Speak Up: Experiences of Inclusive Physical Education', *Disability and Rehabilitation*, 32(18), 1517–1526.

Coates, J. and Vickerman, P. B. (2016), 'Paralympic Legacy: Exploring the Impact of the Games on the Perceptions of Young People with Disabilities', *Adapted Physical Activity Quarterly*, 33(4), 338–357.

Cohen, A., Melton, E. N., and Peachey, J. W. (2014), 'Investigating a Coed Sport's Ability to Encourage Inclusion and Equality', *Journal of Sport Management*, 28(2), 220–235.

Collins, J. (1972), 'The Remedial Hoax', *Remedial Education*, 7(3), 9–10.

Connors, C. and Stalker, K. (2007), 'Children's Experiences of Disability: Pointers to a Social Model of Childhood Disability', *Disability and Society*, 22(1), 19–33.

Corbett, J. and Slee, R. (2000), 'An International Conversation on Inclusive Education', in Armstrong, F., Armstrong, D., and Barton, L. (eds), *Inclusive Education: Policy Contexts and Comparative Perspectives*, David Fulton, London.

Coupe, J. (1986), 'The Curriculum Intervention Model (CIM)', in Coupe, J. and Porter, J. (eds), *The Education of Children with Severe Learning Difficulties: Bridging the Gap Between Theory and Practice*, Croom Helm, London.

Cowne, E. (2005), 'What do Special Educational Needs Coordinators Think They Do?', *British Journal of Learning Support*, 20(2), 61–68.

Craft, D. (1996), 'A Focus on Inclusion in Physical Education', in Hennessy, B. (ed.), *Physical Education Sourcebook*, Human Kinetics, Champaign.

Croll, P. and Moses, M. (2000), 'Ideologies and Utopias: Education Professionals' Views of Inclusion', *European Journal of Special Needs Education*, 15(1), 1–12.

Daniels, H. and Garner, P. (1999), 'Introduction', in Daniels, H. and Garner, P. (eds), *World Yearbook of Education 1999: Inclusive Education*, Kogan Page, London.

DCMS (Department for Culture Media and Sport) (2008), *Playing to Win: A New Era for Sport*, HMSO, London.

Depauw, K. and Doll-Tepper, G. (2000), 'Toward Progressive Inclusion and Acceptance: Myth or Reality? The Inclusion Debate and Bandwagon Discourse', *Adapted Physical Activity Quarterly*, 17, 135–143.

Depauw, K. and Gavron, S. (2005), *Disability and Sport* (2nd edition), Human Kinetics, Champaign.

DES (Department of Education and Science) (1978), *Special Educational Needs: Report of the Committee of Enquiry into the Education of Handicapped Children and Young People (The Warnock Report)*, HMSO, London.

DES (Department of Education and Science) (1981), *The 1981 Education Act*, HMSO, London.

DES (Department of Education and Science) (1984a), *Initial Teacher Training Approval of Courses*, Circular 3/84, HMSO, London.

DES (Department of Education and Science) (1984b), *Initial Teacher Training Approval of Courses*, Circular 24/89, HMSO, London.

DES (Department for Education and Science) (1989), *The Elton Report*, HMSO, London.

DES (Department of Education and Science) (1992a), *Initial Teacher Training Approval of Courses*, Circular 9/92, HMSO, London.

DES (Department of Education and Science) (1992b), *Physical Education in the National Curriculum*, London, HMSO.

Dessent, T. (1987), *Making the Ordinary School Special*, Falmer Press, London.

DfE (Department for Education) (2013a), *Teachers' Standards*, London, HMSO.

DfE (Department for Education) (2013b) *Improving the Quality of Teaching and Leadership*, DfE, London.

DfE (Department for Education) (2014a), *The National Curriculum in England: Key Stages 3 and 4 Framework Document*, London, HMSO.

DfE (Department for Education) (2014b), *Teachers' Standards: How Should They Be Used?* HMSO, London.

DfE (Department for Education) (2014c) 'Get Into Teaching' [online] Available at: www.education.gov.uk/get-into-teaching/teacher-training-options/school-based-training (Accessed 31 August 2017).

DfE (Department for Education) (2014d), *The National Curriculum in England: Key Stages 1 and 2 Framework Document*, HMSO, London.

DfE (Department for Education) (2016) *Educational Excellence Everywhere*, HMSO, London.

DfE (Department for Education) (2017a), *National Statistics: Special Educational Needs and Disability in England*, HMSO, London.

DfE (Department for Education) (2017b), 'What We Do' [online] Available at: www.gov.uk/government/organisations/department-for-education (Accessed 30 August 2017).

DfE/DoH (Department for Education/Department of Health) (2015) *Special Educational Needs and Disability Code of Practice: 0 to 25 Years*, HMSO, London.

DfEE (Department for Education and Employment) (1997a), *Excellence for All Children: Meeting Special Educational Needs*, HMSO, London.

DfEE (Department for Education and Employment) (1997b), *Initial Teacher Training Approval of Courses*, Circular 9/97, HMSO, London.

DfEE (Department for Education and Employment) (1997c), *Teaching: High Status, High Standards – Requirements for Courses of Initial Teacher Training*, Circular 10/97, HMSO, London.

DfES (Department for Education and Skills) (1998a), *Teaching: High Status, High Standards – Requirements for Courses of Initial Teacher Training*, Circular 4/ 98, HMSO, London.

DfES (Department for Education and Skills) (2001a), *Schools Achieving Success*, London, HMSO.

DfES (Department for Education and Skills) (2001b), *Special Educational Needs Code of Practice*, HMSO, London.

DfES (Department for Education and Skills) (2001c), *Special Educational Needs and Disability Act*, HMSO, London.

DfES (Department for Education and Skills) (2004a), *Every Child Matters*, HMSO, London.

DfES (Department for Education and Skills) (2004b), *Statistics of Education: Special Educational Needs in England, January 2000*, Circular 12/01, HMSO, London.

DfES (Department for Education and Skills) and DCMS (Department for Culture, Media and Sport (2002), *Learning through PE and Sport: A Guide to Physical Education, School Sport and Club Links Strategy*, DfES/DCMS, London.

DoE (Department of Education) (1870), *The Education for All Handicapped Children Act (1870)*, HMSO, London.

DoE (Department of Education) (1944), *The Education Act (1944)*, HMSO, London.

DoE (Department of Education) (1970), *The Education (Handicapped Act) 1970*, HMSO, London.

DoE (Department of Education) (1988) *Education Reform Act*, HMSO, London.

DoE (Department of Education) (1994) *Code of Practice on the Identification and Assessment of Special Educational Needs*, HMSO, London.

DoH (Department of Health) (2011), *Start Active, Stay Active*, HMSO, London.

Dunn, L. (1968), 'Special Education for the Mildly Retarded: Is Much of It Justifiable?' *Exceptional Children*, 35, 5–22.

Dyson, A. (1999), 'Issues of Inclusion', unpublished paper, Department of Education, University of Newcastle.

Dyson, A. (2001), 'Special Needs in the Twenty-First Century: Where We've Been and Where we're Going', *British Journal of Special Education*, 28(1), 24–29.

Dyson, A. and Millward, A. (2000), *Issues of Innovation and Inclusion*, Paul Chapman, London.

Earl, L. M. (2012), *Assessment as Learning: Using Classroom Assessment to Maximize Student Learning*, Corwin Press, Thousand Oaks, CA.

EFDS (English Federation for Disability Sport) (2017), 'Our Work' [online] Available at: www.efds.co.uk/about-us/our-work (Accessed 31 August 2017).

Fakolade, O. A., Adeniyi, S. O., and Tella, A. (2017), 'Attitude of Teachers Towards the Inclusion of Special Needs Children in General Education Classroom: The Case of Teachers in some Selected Schools in Nigeria', *International Electronic Journal of Elementary Education*, 1(3), 155–169.

Farr, J. (2018), 'Between a Rock and a Hard Place: The Impact of the Professionalization of the Role of the Teaching Assistant in Mainstream School Physical Education in the United Kingdom, *Sport in Society*, 21(1), 106–124.

Farrell, M. (1998), *The Special Education Handbook*, David Fulton, London.

Farrell, P. (2000), 'The Impact of Research on Developments in Inclusive Education', *International Journal of Inclusive Education*, April, 153–164.

Farrell, P. (2001), 'Special Education in the Last Twenty Years: Have things really got better?' *British Journal of Special Education*, 8(1), 3–9.

Feiler, A. and Gibson, H. (1999), 'Threats to the Inclusive Movement', *British Journal of Special Education*, 26(3), 147–152.

Fitzgerald, H. (2005), 'Still Feeling Like a Spare Piece of Luggage? Embodied Experiences of (Dis)ability in Physical Education and School Sport', *Physical Education & Sport Pedagogy*, 10(1), 41–59.

Fitzgerald, H. (2007), 'Dramatizing Physical Education: Using Drama in Research', *British Journal of Learning Disabilities*, 35, 253–260.

Flecha, R. (2014), *Successful Educational Actions for Inclusion and Social Cohesion in Europe*, Springer, New York.

Florian, L. (eds) (2014), *The SAGE Handbook of Special Education: Volumes 1 and 2*, SAGE, London.

Frapwell, A., Glass, C., and Pearce, L. (2002), 'Assessment: Work in Progress', *British Journal of Teaching Physical Education*, 33, 23–25.

Fredrickson, N. and Cline, T. (2002), *Special Educational Needs, Inclusion and Diversity*, Open University Press, Birmingham.

Fuchs, D. and Fuchs, L. (1994), 'Inclusive Schools Movement and the Radicalisation of Special Education Reform', *Exceptional Children*, 60(4), 294–309.

Galloway, D. and Goodwin, C. (1979), *Educating Slow-Learning and Maladjusted Children: Integration or Segregation*, Longman, London.

Gardiner, J. (1988), 'Functional Aspects of Re-collective Experience', *Memory and Cognition*, 16, 309–313.

Georgeson, J., Porter, J., Daniels, H., and Feiler, A. (2014), 'Consulting Young Children about Barriers and Supports to Learning', *European Early Childhood Education Research Journal*, 22(2), 198–212.

Gerschel, L. (2005), 'The Special Educational Needs Coordinator's Role in Managing Teaching Assistants: The Greenwich Perspective', *Support for Learning*, 20(2), 69–76.

Giangreco, M., Dennis, R., Cloninger, C., Edelman, S., and Schattman, R. (1993), '"I've Counted Jon": Transformational Experiences of Teachers Educating Students with Disabilities', *Exceptional Children*, 59(4), 359–372.

Goodwin, L. and Watkinson, J. (2000), 'Inclusive Physical Education from the Perspectives of Students with Physical Disabilities', *Adapted Physical Activity Quarterly*, 17, 144–160.

Haegele J., Hodge S., Barbosa Gutierres Filho P., and Goncalves de Rezende, A. (2018), 'Brazilian Physical Education Teachers' Attitudes Toward Inclusion Before and After Participation in A Professional Development Workshop', *European Physical Education Review*, 24 (1), 21–38.

Henderson S. Sugden D., and Barnett A. (2007) *Movement Assessment Battery for Children-2* (2nd edition), The Psychological Corporation, London.

Her Majesty's Stationery Office (1998), *The Human Rights Act*, HMSO, London.

Hodge, S., Lieberman, L., and Murata, N. (2017), *Essentials of Teaching Adapted Physical Education: Diversity, Culture and Inclusion*, Routledge, London.

Hodges, C., Jackson, D., Scullion, R. Thompson, S., and Molesworth, M. (2014), *Tracking Changes in Everyday Experiences of Disability and Disability Sport within the Context of the 2012 London Paralympics, Project Report*, CMC Publishing, Bournemouth University, Poole.

Hodkinson, A. (2005), 'Conceptions and Misconceptions of Inclusive Education: A Critical Examination of Final-Year Teacher Trainees' Knowledge and Understanding of Inclusion', *Research in Education*, 73(1), 15–28.

Hutzler, Y., Fliess, O., Chacham, A., and Auweele, Y. (2002), 'Perspectives of Children with Physical Disabilities on Inclusion and Empowerment: Supporting and Limiting Factors', *Adapted Physical Activity Quarterly*, 19, 300–317.

Inner London Education Authority (1985), *Educational Opportunities for All?* (Fish Report), Inner London Education Authority, London.

Jones, P. (2005), 'Teacher's Views of their Pupils with Profound and Multiple Learning Difficulties', *European Journal of Special Needs Education*, 20(4), 375–385.

Joseph Rowntree Foundation (2001), 'Consulting with Disabled Children and Young People' [online] Available at: www.jrf.org.uk/report/consulting-disabled-children-and-young-peo ple (Accessed 22 May 2018).

Kiuppis, F. and Haustatter, R. (eds) (2015), *Inclusive Education Twenty Years After Salamanca*, Peter Lang, Oxford.

Kolb, D. (1976), *The Learning Style Inventory*, McBer, Boston.

Kolb, D. (2014), *Experiential Learning: Experience as a Source of Learning and Development* (2nd edition), Pearson Education, New Jersey.

Kyriacou, C. (1986), *Effective Teaching in Schools*, Blackwell, Oxford.

Laban, R. (1942), *The Mastery of Movement* (4th edition), McDonald and Evans, London.

Lambe, J. (2011), 'Pre-service Education and Attitudes towards Inclusion: The Role of the Teacher Educator within a Permeated Teaching Model', *International Journal of Inclusive Education*, 15(9), 975–999.

Lambe, J. and Bones, R. (2006), 'Student Teacher's Perceptions about Inclusive Classroom Teaching in Northern Ireland prior to Teacher Practice Experience', *European Journal of Special Needs Education*, 21(2), 167–286.

Lipsky, D. and Gartner, A. (1999), *Inclusion and Schools Reform: Transforming America's Classrooms*, Paul H. Brookes, Baltimore.

Lloyd, C. (2000), 'Excellence for all Children – False Promises! The Failure of Current Policy for Inclusive Education and Implications for Schooling in the 21st Century', *International Journal of Inclusive Education*, April, 133–152.

MacConville, R. (2007), *Looking at inclusion: Listening to the Voices of Young People*, Paul Chapman Publishing, London.

Maher, A. (2010) 'The Inclusion of Pupils with Special Educational Needs: A Study of the Formulation and Implementation of the National Curriculum Physical Education in Britain', *Sport Science Review*, XIX (1–2), 87–117.

Maher, A. (2013), 'Statements of Special Educational Needs and Physical Education', *British Journal of Special Education*, 40(3), 131–136.

Maher, A. (2017), '"We've Got a Few Who Don't Go to PE" Learning support assistant and special educational needs coordinator views on inclusion in physical education in England', *European Physical Education Review*, 23(2), 257–270.

Maher, A. (2018), '"Disable them all": SENCO and LSA Conceptualisations of Inclusion in Physical Education', *Sport, Education and Society*, 23(2), 149–161.

Maher, A. and Macbeth, J. (2013), 'Physical Education, Resources and Training: The Perspective of Special Educational Needs Coordinators Working in Secondary Schools in North-West England', *European Physical Education Review*, 20(1), 90–103.

Maher, A., Morley, D., Fimusanmi, J., and Ogilvie, P. (2017), 'The Impact of a Special School Placement on Self-perceptions of Confidence and Competence Among Prospective PE Teachers', *European Physical Education Review* [online first] Available at: http://journals.sagepub.com/doi/abs/10.1177/1356336X17746949 (Accessed 22 May 2018).

Maher, A. and Vickerman, P. (2018), 'Ideology Influencing Action: Special Educational Needs Co-ordinator and Learning Support Assistant Role Conceptualisations and Experiences of Special Needs Education in England', *Journal of Research in Special Educational Needs*, 18(1), 15–25.

Massey, A. (2016), *Provision Mapping and the SEND Code of Practice: Making it Work in Primary, Secondary and Special Schools* (2nd edition), Routledge, London.

Medcalf, R. (2008), *Methodological Considerations; Listening to the Voices of Children with Social Emotional and Behavioural Difficulties in Physical Education*, BERA Annual Student Conference 2008, Heriot Watt University, Edinburgh, UK.

Mihajlovic, C. (2017), 'Pedagogies for Inclusion in Finnish PE: The Teachers' Perspective', *European Journal of Adapted Physical Activity*, 10(2), 36–49.

Mintzberg, H. (1979), *The Structuring of Organisations*, Prentice Hall, New York.

Mintzberg, H. (1983), *Structure in Fives: Designing Effective Organisations*, Prentice Hall, New York.

Mitchell, D. (2014), *What Really Works in Special and Inclusive Education: Using Evidence-Based Teaching Strategies* (2nd edition), Routledge, London.

Mittler, P. (1985), 'Integration: The Shadow and the Substance', *Educational and Child Psychology*, 2(3), 8–22.

Morgan, N. (2016), 'Foreword' In DfE (Department for Education) *Educational Excellence Everywhere*, London, HMSO.

Morley, D., Bailey, R., Tan, J., and Cooke, B. (2005), 'Inclusive Physical Education: Teachers' Views of Including Pupils with Special Educational Needs and/or Disabilities in Physical Education', *European Physical Education Review*, 11(1), 84–107.

Morley, D., Maher, A., Walsh, B., Dinning, T., Lloyd, D., and Pratt, A. (2017), 'Making Reasonable Adjustments for Pupils with Special Educational Needs and Disabilities: Pre-service Teachers' Perceptions of an Online Support Resource', *British Journal of Special Education*, 44(2), 203–219.

Morris, E. (2001) *Professionalism and Trust: A Speech by the Rt. Hon. Estelle Morris MP Secretary of State for Education and Skills to the Social Market Foundation*, HMSO, London.

Mosston, M. and Ashworth, S. (2001), *Teaching Physical Education* (5th edition), Macmillan, London.

Nasen (2014) *Everybody Included: The SEND Code of Practice Explained*, Nasen, Tamworth, UK.

NCTL (National College for Teaching and Leadership) (2014), *National Award for SEN Coordination: Learning Outcomes*, NCTL, London.

NCTL (National College for Teaching and Leadership) (2016), 'Initial Teacher Training Allocations for Academic Year 2015 to 2016' [online] Available at: www.gov.uk/government/publications/initial-teacher-training-allocations-for-academic-year-2015-to-2016 (Accessed 31 August 2017).

NCTL (National College of Teaching and Leadership) (2017), 'About Us' [online] Available at: www.gov.uk/government/organisations/national-college-for-teaching-and-leadership/about (Accessed 30 August 2017).

Newton, A. and Bowler, M. (2010), 'Assessment for and of Learning', in Capel, S. and Whitehead, M. (eds), *Learning to Teach Physical Education in The Secondary School*, Routledge, London.

Norwich, B. (2002a), 'Education, Inclusion and Individual Differences: Recognising and Resolving Dilemmas', *British Journal of Education Studies*, 50(4), 482–502.

Norwich, B. (2008), *Dilemmas of Difference, Inclusion and Disability: International Perspectives and Future Directions*, Routledge, London.

OFSTED (Office for Standards in Education) (2016), *School Inspection Handbook*, OFSTED, London.

OFSTED (Office for Standards in Education) (2017), 'About Us' [online] Available at: www.gov.uk/government/organisations/ofsted/about (Accessed 30 August 2017).

Oliver, M. (1988), 'The Social and Political Context of Educational Policy: The Case of Special Needs', in Barton, L. (ed.), *The Politics of Special Educational Needs*, Falmer, London.

Oliver, M. (1990), *The Politics of Disablement*, Macmillan, London.

Parow, B. (2009), 'Working with Children with Social, Emotional and Behavioural Difficulties: A View from Speech and Language Therapists', *Emotional and Behavioural Difficulties*, 14(4), 301–314.

Pearson, N., Braithwaite, R., Biddle, A., van Sluijs, E., and Atkin, A. (2014), 'Associations between Ssedentary Behaviour and Physical Activity in Children and Adolescents: a Meta-Analysis', *Obesity Reviews*, 15(8), 666–675.

Phillpots, L. (2013), 'An Analysis of the Policy Process for Physical Education and School Sport: The Rise and Demise of School Sport Partnerships, *International Journal of Sport Policy and Politics*, 5(2), 193–211.

Piaget, J. (1962), *Judgement and Reasoning in the Child*, Routledge, London.

Pijl, S., Meijer, C., and Hegarty, S. (eds) (1997), *Inclusive Education: A Global Agenda*, Routledge, London.

Piotrowski, S. (2000), 'Assessment Recording and Reporting', in Bailey, R. and MacFadyen, T. (eds), *Teaching Physical Education 5–11*, Continuum, London.

Place, K. and Hodge, S. (2001), 'Social Inclusion of Students with Physical Disabilities in General Physical Education: A Behavioural Analysis', *Adapted Physical Activity Quarterly*, 18, 389–404.

Pring, R. (1996), 'Just Desert', in Furlong, J. and Smith, R. (eds), *The Role of Higher Education in Initial Teacher Training*, Kogan Page, London.

QCA (Qualification Curriculum Authority) (1999a), *The National Curriculum for England. Physical Education Key Stages 1–4*, QCA, London.

QCA (Qualification Curriculum Authority) (1999c), *The National Curriculum – Handbook for Secondary Teachers in England*, QCA, London.

Reiser, R. and Mason, M. (1990), *Disability Equality in the Classroom: A Human Rights Issue*, Inner London Education Authority, London.

Reynolds, D., Teddlie, C., Hopkins, D., and Stringfield, S. (2000), 'Linking School Effectiveness and School Improvement', in Teddlie, C. and Reynolds, D. (eds), *The International Handbook of School Effectiveness Research*, Falmer Press, London.

Richter, K., Adams-Mushett, C., Ferrara, M., and McCann, B. (1992), 'Integrated Swimming Classification: A Faulted System', *Adapted Physical Activity Quarterly*, 9, 5–13.

Roth, K., Zittel, L., Pyfer, J., and Auxter, D. (2017), *Principles and Methods of Adapted Physical Education and Recreation* (12th edition), McGraw-Hill, New York.

Rouse, M. and Florian, L. (1997), 'Inclusive Education in the Market Place', *International Journal of Inclusive Education*, 1(4), 323–336.

Runswick-Cole, K. (2011) 'Time to End the Bias Towards Inclusive Education?', *British Journal of Special Education*, 38(3), 112–119.

Sato, T. and Haegele, J. A. (2017), 'Graduate Students' Practicum Experiences Instructing Students with Severe and Profound Disabilities in Physical Education', *European Physical Education Review*, 23(2), 196–211.

Sharma, U. and Sokal, L. (2015), 'The Impact of a Teacher Education Course on Pre-Service Teachers' Beliefs about Inclusion: An International Comparison', *Journal of Research in Special Educational Needs*, 15(4), 276–284.

Sherrill, C. (2004), *Adapted Physical Activity, Recreation and Sport* (6th edition), McGraw Hill, Dubuque.

Skrtic, T. (1991), 'The Special Education Paradox: Equity as the Way to Excellence', *Harvard Educational Review*, 61(2), 148–206.

Skrtic, T. (1995), 'The Functionalist View of Special Education and Disability: Deconstructing the Conventional Knowledge Tradition', in Skrtic, T. (ed.), *Disability and Democracy. Reconstructing (Special) Education for Post-modernity*, Teachers College Press, New York.

Slininger, D., Sherrill, C., and Jankowski, C. (2000), 'Children's Attitudes Towards Peers with Severe Disabilities: Revisiting Contact Theory', *Adapted Physical Activity Quarterly*, 17, 176–198.

Smith, A. and Green, K. (2004), 'Including Pupils with Special Educational Needs in Secondary School Physical Education: A Sociological Analysis of Teachers' Views', *British Journal of Sociology of Education*, 25(5), 593–608.

Snowling, M. (2012), 'Early Identification and Interventions for Dyslexia: A Contemporary View', *Journal of Research in Special Educational Needs*, 13(1), 7–14.

Sonday, A. and Gretschel, P. (2016), 'Empowered to Play: A Case Study Describing the Impact of Powered Mobility on the Exploratory Play of Disabled Children', *Occupational therapy International*, 23(1), 11–18.

Sparkes, A., Martos-Garcia, D., and Maher, A. (2017) 'Me, Osteogenesis Imperfecta, and my Classmates in Physical Education Lessons: A Case Study of Embodied Pedagogy in Action', *Sport, Education and Society* [online first] Available at: www.tandfonline.com/doi/full/10.108 0/13573322.2017.1392939 (Accessed 22 May 2018).

Sport England (1997), *Task Force on the Future of Disability Sport*, Sport England, London.

Sport England (2016), *Towards an Active Nation*, Sport England, London.

Sport England (2017), 'Evaluation of Satellite Clubs: Final Report' [online] Available at: www. sportengland.org/media/11778/sport-england-evaluation-of-satellite-clubs-final-report-executive-summary-june-2017.pdf (Accessed 24 January 2018).

Sugden, D. and Henderson. S. (1994), 'Help with Movement', *Special Children*, 75, 1–8.

Sugden D. and Talbot, M. (1998), *Physical Education for Children with Special Needs in Mainstream Education*, Carnegie National Sports Development Centre, Leeds.

Szwed, C. (2007), 'Remodelling Policy and Practice: The Challenge for Staff Working with Children with Special Educational Needs', *Educational Review*, 59(2), 147–60.

Tansley, A. and Guidford, R. (1960), *The Education of Slow Learning Children* (2nd edition), Routledge and Kegan Paul, London.

Tant, M. and Watelain, E. (2016), 'Forty Years Later, A Systematic Literature Review on Inclusion in Physical Education (1975–2015): A Teacher Perspective', *Educational Research Review*, 19, 1–17.

Tomlinson, S. (1982), *A Sociology of Special Education*, Routledge and Kegan Paul, London.

Tomlinson, S. (1985), 'The Expansion of Special Education', *Oxford Review of Education*, (2), 157–165.

TTA (Teacher Training Agency) (1998a), *Framework for the Assessment of Quality and Standards in Teacher Training*, Circular 4/98, Teacher Training Agency, London.

TTA (Teacher Training Agency) (2002), *Qualifying to Teach. Professional Standards for Qualified Teacher Status and Requirements for Initial Teacher Training*, Circular 02/02 (TTA 2002), Teacher Training Agency, London.

UCET (Universities Council for the Education of Teachers) (1997a), *Initial Teacher Education: TTA/OFSTED Quality Framework: A Critique*. Occasional Paper Number November, UCET, London.

UN (United Nations) (1992), *Convention on the Rights of the Child* [online] Available at: www2. ohchr.org/english/law/crc.htm (Accessed 2 March 2018).

UNESCO (United Nations Educational, Scientific, and Cultural Organization) (1994), *The Salamanca Statement and Framework for Action on Special Needs Education*, Salamanca, UNESCO.

UNISON (2013), 'The Evident Value of Teaching Assistants' [online] Available at: www.unison.org. uk/upload/sharepoint/Briefings%20and%20Circulars/EVIDENT%20VALUE%20OF%20 TEACHING%20ASSISTANTS%20%28Autosaved%29.pdf (Accessed 16 October 2017).

United States of America Federal Government (1975), *Public Law 94–142, Education for All Handicapped Children*, US Federal Government, Washington DC.

Vickerman, P. (2002), 'Perspectives on the Training of Physical Education Teachers for the Inclusion of Children with Special Educational Needs: Is There an Official Line View?' *Bulletin of Physical Education*, 38(2), 79–98.

Vickerman, P. (2007), 'Training Physical Education Teachers to Include Children with Special Educational Needs: Perspectives from Physical Education Teacher Training Providers' *European Physical Education Review* 18(3), 285–402.

Vickerman, P. (2010), 'Planning for an Inclusive Approach to Learning and Teaching', in Capel, S. and Whitehead, M. (eds), *Learning to Teach Physical Education in the Secondary School* (3rd edition), Routledge, London.

Vickerman, P. and Coates, J. (2009), 'Trainee and Recently Qualified Physical Education Teachers' Perspectives on Including Children with Special Educational Needs' *Physical Education and Sport Pedagogy* 14(2), 137–153.

Vickerman, P. and Hayes, S. (2013), 'Special Educational Needs and Disability in Physical Education', in Stidder, G. and Hayes, S. (eds), *Equity and Inclusion in Physical Education*, Routledge, London.

Vickerman, P. and Maher, A. (2017), 'A Holistic Approach to Training for Inclusion in Physical Education: Policy, Practice, Challenges and Solutions' In Morin, A., Maiano, C., Tracey, D., and R. Craven (eds), *Inclusive Physical Activities: International Perspectives*, Information Age Publishing, Charlotte, NC.

Vincent, C., Evans, J., Lunt, I., Steedman, J., and Wedell, K. (1994), 'The Market Forces? The Effect of Local Management on Special Educational Needs Provision', *British Educational Research Journal*, 20(3), 261–278.

Vislie, L. and Langfeldt, G. (1996), 'Finance, Policy Making and the Organisation of Special Education', *Cambridge Journal of Education*, 26(1), 59–70.

Volger, E. and Romance, T. (2000), 'Including a Child with Severe Cerebral Palsy in Physical Education: A Case Study', *Adapted Physical Activity Quarterly*, 17, 161–182.

Vygotsky, L. (1962), *Thought and Language*, MIT Press, Cambridge.

Wang, Y. (2016), *Imagining Inclusive Schooling: An Ethnographic Inquiry into Disabled Children's Learning and Participation in Regular Schools in Shanghai.* Unpublished PhD Thesis, University of Edinburgh, Edinburgh.

Weddell, K. (2004) 'Points from the SENCO-Forum: Life as a SENCO', *British Journal of Special Education*, 31(3), 105.

Weddell, K. (2008), 'Confusion about Inclusion: Patching Up or System Change?' *British Journal of Special Education*, 35(3), 127–135.

Wilhelmsen, T. and Sørensen, M. (2017), 'Inclusion of Children with Disabilities in Physical Education: A Systematic Review of Literature From 2009 to 2015', *Adapted Physical Activity Quarterly*, 34(3), 311–337.

Winnick, J. (1987), 'An Integration Continuum for Sport Participation', *Adapted Physical Activity Quarterly*, 4, 157–161.

Winnick, J. (2000), *Adapted Physical Education and Sport* (3rd edition), Human Kinetics, Leeds.

Winnick, J. and Porretta, D. (2017), *Adapted Physical Education and Sport* (6th edition), Human Kinetics, Leeds.

Woolfson, R., Harker, M., Lowe, D., Shields, M., and Mackintosh, H. (2007), 'Consulting with Children and Young People who have Disabilities: Views of Accessibility to Education', *British Journal of Special Education*, 34(1), 40–49.

YST (Youth Sport Trust) (2017a), 'Sainsbury's Active Kids For All Inclusive PE' [online] Available at: www.youthsporttrust.org/sainsbury%E2%80%99s-active-kids-all-inclusive-pe (Accessed 1 September 2017).

YST (Youth Sport Trust) (2017b), 'TOP Sportsability' [online] Available at: www.youthsporttrust.org/top-sportsability (Accessed 1 September 2017).

Index